1691

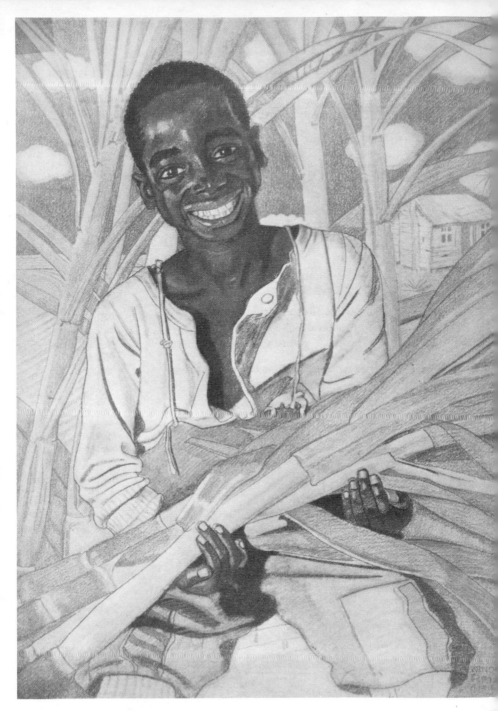

Anthony, just in from the sugar-cane patch.

School Acres

An Adventure in Rural Education

By

Rossa B. Cooley

Principal, Penn Normal, Industrial and
Agricultural School, St. Helena Island
South Carolina

Illustrated with crayons from life by
Winold Reiss

With an Introduction by Paul U. Kellogg
Editor, "The Survey," New York

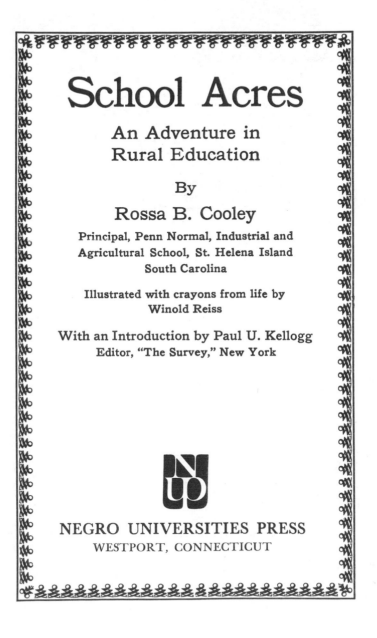

NEGRO UNIVERSITIES PRESS
WESTPORT, CONNECTICUT

Originally published in 1930
by Yale University Press, New Haven

Reprinted in 1970 by
Negro Universities Press
A Division of Greenwood Press, Inc.
Westport, Connecticut

Library of Congress Catalogue Card Number 71-106853

SBN 8371-3475-7

Printed in the United States of America

To

The Girls and Boys of the Sea Islands

who are preparing themselves for the responsibilities
of their inheritance and to

Their Teachers

I dedicate this book

INTRODUCTION

Throughout the pages of "School Acres" we catch glimpses of the white oyster-shell roads which, like shining threads, knit the plantation life of St. Helena Island into a community, and thus symbolize the genius of Penn School. Down those roads a pageant of civilization unrolls before us as on a scroll.

For seldom has an educational experiment had such a setting. The epoch of the war between the states hangs like a backdrop. In the tidal rivers of these islands off the coast of South Carolina the last of the slave ships discharged their cargoes of primitive Africans, bootlegged across the Atlantic long after the outlawry of the trade. On these great plantations, sea-island cotton was grown under conditions that epitomized the extremes of agricultural mass-production under forced labor. It was here, during the early years of the war, with the islands occupied by Union forces, that the first attempts were made to employ Negro cotton growers at wages. And it was here that emancipation first reached the southern cotton lands and beginnings were made by Negro freeholders on their own small plots. We are told that Lincoln's thinking on the question of how to deal with the freedmen was influenced by what went forward in this occupied zone.

In such a setting then this first southern Negro
school was opened in the early sixties, its founders
demonstrating that these field hands, marooned in ig-
norance under slavery, would respond to teaching. And
against this background, under their successors, Rossa
B. Cooley and Grace Bigelow House, that belated liberty and that early learning have been linked with life.

Our scroll stretches wide in the midst of this process.
Things spanned in a thousand years are compressed
into decades. We catch glimpses of a transit in three
generations from unlettered superstition to responsive
and discriminating play of intelligence. We watch
the shift from conjuror and charms to island doctor
and nurse and clinic—the swift incursion and adaptation of modern advances in medicine and health work.
We look across old fields, hitherto tilled much as hus-
bandmen of the Old Testament tilled theirs, as these
yield to scientific advances in soil building and to modern ways and tools. We see the issue joined between
the old one-crop system that still binds the South and a
revolutionary program of food crops and rotation; we
see the unequal contest between isolated small farmers
and the modern truck farm, and the hope held out for
them by coöperative credit and marketing, here first
instituted in South Carolina. We sense realistic forces
that counter the cityward migration by enriching the
life of a countryside; and, bit by bit, there is borne in
upon us the creative significance implicit in the work
of Penn School—a significance that reaches beyond the

school's very tangible contribution to the well-being of its island setting.

St. Helena has become a laboratory where for a quarter of a century has been carried out our most arresting experiment in community education. And while Miss Cooley tells the story of it in a way that makes the pageantry of those oyster-shell roads pass before us, with its color and incident and personality, she has blended with her narrative a record of practical experience that will be of help to race leaders and rural educators everywhere. Every year has brought more of them to the island to study this living exhibit. In the guest book at Penn the place names range from mission posts on the Congo to schools in the hinterland of India, from Appalachian crossroads to the traveling educational missions of Mexico. A wall map of Africa is dotted with pins, each standing for the home station of some visitor to Penn. Dr. Thomas Jesse Jones, who has headed the educational commissions sent by the Phelps Stokes Fund throughout that continent, has spread the story of these sea islands among those who would recast missionary enterprise in modern terms. And Sir Gordon Guggisberg found on his visit to Penn the most convincing example in America of the practicability of what he was driving at as governor of the Gold Coast, when he set out to rebuild colonial administration on the basis of racial revival. For on these mud flats have taken root the imaginative proposals of such men as Armstrong and Frissell, Seaman Knapp

and Horace Plunkett. The educational principles which
have been promoted at Hampton and Tuskegee and the
other great centers of vocational training have not only
been brought to earth on St. Helena, but they have
been broadened into a quickening scheme of service to
life as a whole.

There is something primal in the rediscovery of the
power of the school as a social dynamo. This finds expression at Penn in its all-year rhythm, its island-wide
reach, its awareness of the all-round wants and urges
and aspirations of simple folk; its release of the organic
strength of the community, and its stirring frontage on
change.

Last summer, I visited some of the mountain districts back of the Mexican plateau where the cultural
missions of the Federal Department of Education are
at work. They stimulate and supervise the village
schools, often erected by the villagers themselves.
These reach men, women, and children alike; village
orchestras and crude theaters under the trees of the
school yard minister to people who had been starved
of the spirit as well as the body under the "hacienda"
system. The schools are centers for all manner of enter-
prises in the interests of health and of industrial and
agricultural rehabilitation. Alfalfa fields are plowed
and harvested in common; blacksmith shops and tan-
neries are improvised; joint projects in improving live
stock go forward. These coöperative ventures stimu-
lated by the schools give young and old a sense of push-

ing up and out from their former stagnant levels of existence, gird their mutual strength in confronting new days. Feeding into them are normal schools, tenants often of monasteries unused for a century. These equip young teachers for leadership not merely with book learning, but with working knowledge of the characteristics of nearby soils, of the virtues of native plants for dyeing and tanning and for the cure of the sick, and of the uses of those raw materials and simple tools by which a countryside may help to pull itself up by its own bootstraps.

Small wonder that I learned that leaders among them had drawn from Hampton and Tuskegee, had visited Penn, just as the American Farm School at Salonika, Greece, has drawn from these American institutes in its pioneering in agricultural and industrial education in the Balkans; and Penn in turn has drawn from Salonika in organizing its scheme of practical study (see Appendix). While the Mexican leaders I talked with were confident of the future of their rural education, they were baffled when it came to paralleling it in their cities. There the teaching staffs are many of them fixed in the old ruts; the parents have the old stereotypes of what education should be and want their children to go through the old rigmaroles. In the rural work the new leadership is fortunate in having a clean sheet on which to write some of the things that have been learned in the art and scope of teaching since the days of quill pens and slate pencils.

This contrast, which stands out so baldly in Mexico, has its counterpart in the United States. The experience of Penn in education "of the people, by the people, for the people" not only plays luminously on the needs of rural districts the country over, but upon a dilemma confronting our cities. Miss Cooley reveals how the New England school of the "three R's" with its academic ramifications fell short when it came to training-for-life under the changing conditions of the rural South. She sets forth the strategy and spirit of the two revolutions at Penn School—how the life of the farms was brought into the classrooms, and then how through the school acres and other extramural activities the process was reversed and the educational impulse was spread to the ends of the island. And in so doing, she knocks at our city gates. She offers a new approach to the urban teacher or civic leader. In our industrial centers work for children must be realigned to changes far more rapid than those taking place in the country. Moreover, if education means preparation for life, it must be related to the needs of adult men and women striving to keep abreast of those changes. Somehow or other we must match the new stresses which scientific and mechanical advance put on human nature with a social structure at once tough enough and flexible enough to encounter them successfully. Otherwise democracy as we know it will go under beneath the weight of this new mechanization and the great formations in which it takes shape.

From this angle, Penn School is an experiment in re-
leasing initiatives and in fostering coöperative self-reli-
ance in times of change. That the stage in which it is
set is small, the tempo of life comparatively slow, is an
advantage to those who would learn from it; just
as slowed-down moving pictures, which space the
changes gradually enough so that the eye can follow,
help us in studying the motions of the human body.

Fortunately, there have been writings that throw
light on various aspects and decades of the evolution of
the islands. Col. Thomas Wentworth Higginson in his
"Story of a Black Regiment," the "Diary and Letters
of Laura M. Towne," the founder of the school, and
"Port Royal Letters" treat of the early period which
Miss Cooley takes up in her first chapter. The late A. E.
Gonzales, editor of the Columbia "State," was a life-
long student of the Gullah Negroes of this coastal region, and Du Bose Heyward and Julia Peterkin have
made them subjects for fiction. Miss House has herself
written intimate sketches of her neighbors on St.
Helena. "Black Yeomanry" by T. J. Woofter, Jr., and
his associates (Henry Holt & Co., 1930) crystallizes the
findings of the recent sociological survey of the island
people carried out under grant from the Social Science
Research Council by the Institute for Research in Social Science at the University of North Carolina. The
canvas of island life is painted with sure and colorful
strokes and the findings of special branches of the in-
quiry will be published elsewhere and at greater

length. Let me quote Dr. Woofter, himself a south-
erner, on "The Worth of the Experiment"—as he calls
his final chapter:

One can hardly fail to speculate on the probable improvement in the Southern racial situation if the whole area had
been dotted with Penn Schools.

The demonstration of the improvability of health, family
welfare, economic activity, and religion,—the fundamentals
of life,—has been so convincing that other Southern counties
could well afford to assume as government functions some of
the semi-private activities of Penn School. Public health nursing, farm demonstration, home demonstration, and the teaching of agriculture, have all come to be recognized as legiti-
mate government activities in rural districts. The problem of
the South is to discover the people and develop the means to
make these functions as effective for Negroes as for white
people; and as effective for both races in all areas as they are
on the Island.

Nor is the value of the St. Helena experiment confined to
the United States. In Asia, Africa, and the Near East, civi-
lized governments are confronted with the problems of dealing with masses of backward people. These people derive
their incomes from agriculture, and their satisfactions from
rural life. Here the most efficient form which paternalism can
assume is the development of the masses in the fundamental
activities of life. This comes through the sponsorship and
finance of organizations capable of stimulating these essential
functions. In this task government and private philanthropy
have a divided responsibility.

If missionary activity means the fuller development of the
capabilities of a backward people, then the social objectives
of the missionaries and the paternalistic mandate and colonial

governments are the same. Striking examples of successful
methods and policies are to be found for both groups in this
experiment of the development of the St. Helena community.

But Miss Cooley herself has been the outstanding
interpreter both of the school and of the islanders. She
reveals Penn's impact on the island life not as a gesture
of paternalism but as an overture of leadership to release nascent forces for self-development and group initiative. Its genius has been, she shows us, not to lay
things on but to stir things up and build from the bottom democratically. To this end she has interpreted the
islanders to themselves. That after all was the first step
to be taken in the nurture of a new community life. She
has done this in talks made from Land's End to Coffin's
Point; in crossroad school and country church, in fair
and festival, and above all in her friendly rendezvous
with them in their fields and island homes. She has interpreted the islanders to others in annual reports
that have carried the message of Penn to friends
everywhere, and in addresses made in a score of our
American cities. More intimately, she interpreted them
throughout the years in letters to her mother. These,
fortunately, were saved and proved in a special sense a
"Barrel of Gold" in preparing the two books in which
she has set down, piece by piece, the mosaic of island
life. They enabled her to recapture, with the freshness
of current experience, the impulses and incidents that
marked the whole course of her island experience and
the growth of the school's work.

In "Homes of the Freed" (New Republic Press) she set forth for the first time the stages through which three generations of Negro women have worked their way up from the slave street. To pictures of "the peasant woman tugging at the plow rope of the old serf lands of Europe" and "the Indian woman carrying tepee and papoose," she added, in the "gallery of human struggle," the picture of "the Negro woman with the heavy cord tied round her hips to 'give her strenth,' with her baby in her arms and her bundle on her head." But above all she bore witness

to the new generation as they have carried themselves under conditions where they have had a chance to show the stuff that is in them. This may help others to see life as these girls have had to come at it, the lay of some of their chief obstacles, the way to overcome them. It may help others to understand that while the ancient occupations of womenfolk remain their charge, the gauge that freedom set to these Negro women of the southern countrysides was not to become housemaids to be had for wages by city dwellers; but to become the home-makers and mothers and farm women for their own rural communities.

In "School Acres," Miss Cooley tells the story of the school itself. Chapters from both books appeared first serially in "Survey Graphic," and we have considered them among our most unique contributions to the transcript of American social life and adventure.

Last winter, the quarter century which Miss Cooley and Miss House have spent in their island work was celebrated at an informal dinner at Town Hall in New

York. The gathering personified the interests engaged
by the work at Penn: Quakers, who carried the living
tradition back to the days of the founders; men and
women who have spent their lives in rural education in
the South and the urban work of the northern centers;
outstanding white Southerners and leaders of the Negro race; experts in the industrial arts, in rural and
agricultural education from various centers; with C. F.
Andrews, Gandhi's associate in India, standing for
overseas friends on four continents. The meeting was
not only in ardent recognition of an extraordinary span
of work, but those present were united in feeling that
the great foundations might well put adequate funds at
the disposal of this island laboratory as a reinforce-
ment to community education everywhere.

But it was in jasmine time last spring, in the Community House which had grown out of the "Pile of
Faith" at Penn, that the islanders themselves celebrated the twenty-five years during which Miss Cooley
and Miss House have worked among them, sharing
their vicissitudes; undaunted, enduring, carrying the
gleam. And really to know that work, you must see
Miss House in her swift sensing of the drama of an island home, whether that little two-roomed one in the
field, or a prize winner in a national competition; see
her at her desk, where the shuttles of island life run
through the warp and woof of the school administration. To know that work, you must see Miss Cooley in
the saddle, in her intimate encounters with her neigh-

bors, and catch the response as she kindles some great gathering of men and women or children at Darrah Hall or at the Farmers' Fair. There is a give and take to it that stands out in every chapter of this book—that "togetherness" without which any social experiment, however buoyantly conceived, is leaden. She is an islander among them. As she points out, hers is a country of tidal creeks and marshes. Sidney Lanier sang of their like. She tells the story of the people. Hers is a country which, in its look and in the spiritual life that overlays it, is reminiscent of the Bible lands. And she tells the story of its people in ways that have a parable-like quality, so close-in are they and pithy with human experience. At the same time, she tells it in ways that carry the struggle, the sustained purpose, and the zest of the moving pageant of the oyster-shell roads.

PAUL U. KELLOGG

New York City,
    September, 1930.

ACKNOWLEDGMENT

It is natural to dedicate this book to the boys and girls of the sea islands and to their teachers, for they have made the school of today what it is, and they have worked out the problems, as we have met them, in a splendidly loyal and coöperative spirit. And I want to thank the parents, who have been in all of the movement too, as the story shows, for to them I feel a deep debt of gratitude.

Without the help and encouragement of Mr. Paul U. Kellogg I should never have attempted to tell this story. He gladly listened while I read the hundreds of letters my mother had filed away in a tin box for safe-keeping, which told of all the early years on the island. He showed me how to classify and to use them, and "The Survey" accepted the articles which have been incorporated in this book.

I wish also to thank Mrs. Kellogg who helped me prepare the manuscript for the publisher, and to acknowledge the courtesy of Charles Scribner's Sons in granting permission to reprint the selections from "The Marshes of Glynn" and "Sunrise" in the poems of Sidney Lanier.

And to Miss Isabella Curtis, who made it possible for Mr. Winold Reiss to come to St. Helena and make the portraits which are used as illustrations, and to Miss

Grace Bigelow House, the partner in all the plans, who has helped on every mile of the road to interpret the changes to the people, I would express my deep appreciation.

R. B. C.

St. Helena Island,
  South Carolina,
  June 1, 1930.

CONTENTS

ILLUSTRATIONS

PART I

A MISSION OF LOVE AND LITERACY

HERE'S the first bell!" Boys and girls drop their work in the fields as it peals out across the plantations. They join others already on the road. Groups from all directions stream in to be on hand when the second bell calls them to the classrooms. This Liberty Bell at Penn, the oldest school for Negroes in the South, rings every day and many times a day. When the wind is right it can be heard for three miles and it tells the time for nearby folk. It starts off the farm work at seven in the morning; it rings for the men in the fields at twelve; it "knocks them off" at five. For the children, it rings for school and work and play. It used to ring for the neighboring churches on Sunday until they secured their own bells; and when there is an evening entertainment at our Community Building it rings out thrice to tell the people that the time is speeding and they must hurry along the oyster-shell roads.

Every time it rings it carries the message of its inscription, "Proclaim Liberty." That was the message of the founder of Penn School, Laura M. Towne, who came to the sea islands off the coast of South Carolina in the spring of 1862, not long after their capture by the northern forces. With her associate, Ellen Murray, she started on their road to learning the people of St. Helena, one of the islands that shut Beaufort from the sea.

Three generations have responded to the clang of the Liberty Bell. On the front seats in Chapel sit the "grands" of the slaves who first came under its spell. Not only have the people grown, but the living concept for which the school stands has grown. Before the war between the states, work stood for slavery in the minds of the slaves; freedom meant getting away from all manual labor. Liberty meant learning. And in that fact lay the significance of the work of the pioneers who brought education to our southern communities. But in that fact lay the tragedy that as years went on, the gap between the working life of the people and the book learning of the schools widened, as in truth it widened throughout our entire educational system in the United States. We are only now in the process of bridging the two.

In a sense there have been three revolutions in the school-keeping at Penn.

First came the founders, who broke ground and proved that field hands of the cotton lands could learn. We have all but forgotten the deep-reaching insurgency involved in what they set out to do, in the face of the prejudices not only of the plantation owners, but of many of the northerners whom the war brought to the southern coast. The story of the things these pioneers struggled for at Penn runs for forty years.

The later revolutions have been swifter. For as time went on, the limitations of purely academic education became etched deeply in the life of the island. They are the same limitations that are to be found, repeated over and over again, in the average Negro school in the rural South. They are the same limitations which mark the general run of rural schools the country over; the same limitations which mark much of the work of the mission schools in foreign lands which have taken over too faithfully the models of our traditional schooling; the same limitations which in various guises have confronted elementary and high schools and colleges everywhere. So there may be significance to others in the story of how, at the end of those forty years, principles of vocational education developed at Hampton Institute were carried over into the island work; how in ten years we brought the farms to the school. That was the second revolution.

And then—a third phase—the story of the succeeding years, when we in turn have been pioneering at Penn itself, and have been carrying out an experiment which is being watched by educators with mounting interest, bringing the school to the farms, and making this oldest of Negro schools in a sense the newest—an all-island school, an all-the-year-round school, merging school and community into a common adventure.

The story of these three revolutions I shall set down for those who would profit both by our mistakes and by our measure of success.

II

When the Liberty Bell "rang in the new" in the early sixties, the "scholars" of that first school for freedom trooped in, men, women, and children. In the little cabin meetings held in the late evenings on the plantations had been born and sung the old spiritual,

> I know I would like to read,
> Like to read,
> Like to read dat sweet story ob ole,
> I would like to read
> Like to read,
> Like to read dat sweet story ob ole,
> I would like to read.

And at last their chance had come! It is no wonder the school was crowded. It is no wonder that the grandparents came, that the mothers carried their babies to the little classroom, for the spiritual had knit itself into the warp and woof of their lives.

The traditional view that the field hands could be taught only with the whip became a spur to the newly imported teachers. Their motley group of pupils were hungry for learning, and they made it their first rule to have no whip in their school. But before telling of that first revolution they wrought let me give you a glimpse of the people they wrought with and through, from the diary of one of our great interpreters of American life, who was thrown with them in war time.

The first Negroes to step off the island and out from the conditions of slavery were the men recruited in 1862 for the so-called "Hunter Regiment." In the opening year of the war between the states a Union fleet had captured the coast region about Beaufort, had taken over the sea islands and had set out to organize the plantation hands as a military measure. When the measure seemed doomed to failure, General Saxton gave the command to Col. Thomas Wentworth Higginson and in his "Army Life in a Black Regiment," he gives us a picture of his men. Suddenly turned from slaves into soldiers, dressed conspicuously as to their legs in scarlet,* looked upon as a most doubtful experiment, and they themselves looking upon their new experience with suspicion, their imaginations poisoned with false tales as to their use in the war, everything and all things seemed unfavorable. They did not need the trousers to focus the eyes of the country upon them! The newspapers of the time show how every move was watched and commented upon.

* General Hunter had requested this from the Secretary of War, saying, "It is important that I should be able to know and distinguish these men at once." Surely he left no room for doubts!

But interesting as that part of their history is, I am recalling it solely from the viewpoint of the educator. What did this war-time experience show as to the stuff that was in them? Colonel Higginson pictures them as a happy, rollicking lot of men, earnest and grave during drill, delighted with their new discipline and with all the pageantry of war; conscientious and dependable. Story-telling around the camp fire was a favorite pastime, and then as in their games and in their singing, they revealed those dramatic powers which give their race ability to grasp new situations quickly and make them their own. To quote Colonel Higginson:

> Strolling in the cool moonlight, I was attracted by a brilliant light beneath the trees, and cautiously approached it. A circle of thirty or forty soldiers sat around a roaring fire, while one old uncle, Cato by name, was narrating an interminable tale, to the insatiable delight of his audience.— It was a narrative dramatized to the last degree, of his adventures in escaping from his master to the Union vessels; and I, though I had heard the stories of Harriet Tubman, and such wonderful slave comedians, never witnessed such a piece of acting.*

Colonel Higginson retells Cato's story, how he reached the riverside, how he tried to decide whether the vessels held friends or foes, his acts of caution, his foresight, his patient cunning, his tricks, "beyond Molière himself."

And all this to a bivouac of Negro soldiers, with the brilliant fire lighting up their red trousers and gleaming from

* Selections on this page and following pages from Thomas Wentworth Higginson's "Army Life in a Black Regiment," pp. 15, 17–18, 32–33, 374, are quoted by the courteous permission of the publishers, Houghton Mifflin Company, Boston, Massachusetts.

their shining black faces, eyes and teeth all white with tumultuous glee. Overhead the mighty limbs of a great live oak, with the weird moss swaying in the smoke, and the high moon gleaming faintly through. Yet tomorrow strangers will remark on the hopeless, impenetrable stupidity in the daylight faces of many of these very men, the solid mask under which Nature has concealed all this wealth of mother-wit. This very comedian is one to whom one might point, as he hoed lazily in a cotton field, as a being the light of whose brain had utterly gone out.—This is their university. Every young Sambo before me, as he turned over the sweet potatoes and peanuts which were roasting in the ashes, listened with reverence to the wiles of the ancient Ulysses, and meditated the same. It is Nature's compensation; oppression simply crushes the upper faculties of the head, and crowds everything into the perceptive organs. Cato, thou reasonest well! When I get into any serious scrape, in an enemy's country, may I be lucky enough to have you at my elbow to pull me out of it!

The new experiences, tumbling over each other in their rapidity of action, gave these children of the race a new chance to grow. The perceptive powers which Colonel Higginson remarked, unfolded their latent intelligence more rapidly than their commander—or even their first teachers—dared to hope.

A month later Colonel Higginson wrote of another stroll among the camp fires, and again I shall quote from his diary:

Beside some of these fires the men are cleaning their guns or rehearsing their drill; beside others, smoking in silence their very scanty supply of the beloved tobacco; beside others, telling stories, and shouting with laughter over the broadest mimicry, in which they excel, and in which the officers come in for their full share. The everlasting "shout" is always within hearing, with its mixture of piety and polka, and its castanet-like clapping of the hands. Then there are quieter prayer meetings, with pious invocations and slow psalms, "deaconed out" from memory by the leader, two lines at a time, in a sort of a wailing chant. Elsewhere there are "conversazioni" around fires, with a woman for queen of the circle, her Nubian face, gay head-dress, gilt necklace, and white teeth, all resplendent in the glowing light. Sometimes the woman is spelling slow monosyllables out of a primer, a feat which always commands all ears, they rightly recognizing a mighty spell, equal to the overthrowing of monarchs, in the magic assonance of "cat," "hat," "pat," "bat" and the rest of it.

When Colonel Higginson visited the South fourteen years later he found the men and women in their own fields, furniture in their homes, pictures from illustrated papers on the walls, and children's schoolbooks on the shelf. There was a general absence of poverty among them. Of the hundred men who had been under his command and whose peace-time condition he investigated, the single exception was a man without wife or children whose failure was due to whiskey. The returned officer found that the colored population valued the schools which had put book learning within their reach. He wrote:

Public officials in Beaufort [the town nearest St. Helena Island], told me that in that place most of the men could now sign their names,—certainly a great proof of progress since war times. I found some of my friends anxious lest school should unfit the young people for the hard work of the field; but I saw no real proof of this, nor did the parents confirm it.

III

When the group of sea islands became Union territory on November 7, 1861, the northern forces found on their hands not only several thousand Negroes who had hitherto worked only under overseers, but far-reaching acres of long-staple cotton which was of great value. Cotton agents were rushed to the islands to organize the masterless labor force of the plantations and

salvage the crop. Civilian volunteers, women as well
as men, went down to help feed and clothe and teach
the people, just as in the World War our Red Cross,
Quaker, and other contingents went overseas to work
among the refugees back of the front and in the devas-
tated regions. The voyage on a government transport
taken in the sixties by northern teachers seemed quite
as hazardous; and to their families the distance seemed
even greater. Moreover, the islands were known to be
very unhealthy, smallpox was a frequent visitor, the
Confederate army had retreated only a short distance
on the mainland and might return at any time. They
were setting out for a region where, since the flight of
the white masters, there were few besides Negroes; a
race then practically unknown to them, who were
likely to view their coming with suspicion.

Miss Towne chose these hardships to the war-time
hospital service for which she had fitted herself in her
native city of Philadelphia. She first "footed" St.
Helena Island on April 15, 1862, and her diary tells of
the great confusion she found there. Her close friend,
an Englishwoman, Ellen Murray, joined her, and together they added school-teaching to the many duties
of their day, first in the front room of the Oaks Plantation House, which was then the government head-
quarters. The "scholars" soon overflowed onto the
porch, and the school was moved to the neighboring
Brick Church, where in September it numbered eighty
men, women, boys, and girls. Miss Towne described
her first class in a few terse words:

> They had no idea of sitting still, of giving attention, of
> ceasing to talk aloud. They lay down and went to sleep; they
> scuffled and struck each other. They got up by the dozen and
> made their curtsies, and walked off to the neighboring fields
> for blackberries, coming back to their seats with a curtsy

when they were ready. They evidently did not understand me, and I could not understand them, and after two hours and a half of effort I was thoroughly exhausted.

Later, the Pennsylvania Freedmen's Association sent down a schoolhouse in sections and the two self-constituted school-teachers had it put up opposite the Brick Church and named for William Penn, who preached liberty for all. Their charges marched across the road and took their seats in the first schoolhouse for the Negroes in the South.

These grown-up pupils of the war time could count on their fingers up to ten; they did not know how to open a book; they had never been off the island, they knew of no towns but Beaufort and Charleston, and "Sous Carolina" was the world to them. Under an old state law of 1834, it was a crime to teach slaves to read or write. This law had not been enforced and numbers of the house slaves had been taught by their owners, but the privilege was never extended to the field hands who made up most of the island population, and the view as to their ability, held by their southern masters, was echoed by some of the northerners sent down to handle the plantations and in "Letters from Port Royal" we find their frequent expressions of despair and exasperation—even to one sweeping denunciation of the "imbecile character of the people." In a letter of 1863, William C. Gannett wrote:

Their state of morals I should say is decidedly better than it was under slavery, less of licentiousness, lying and stealing, and more general manliness and self-respect. But they are very far behind in character as well as intelligence and I suspect that most abolitionist views of their character are exaggerated in their favor. It increases the need and it does not decrease the interest in helping them, to think so.*

* "Letters from Port Royal," ed. Elizabeth Ware Pearson, and quoted by her courteous permission.

Mr. Gannett was one of the early volunteers who not only served as a superintendent on the cotton plantations, but later shared in the school-teaching, too, and his realistic but hopeful front well expresses the spirit in which the work was entered upon. But let me put the complex problem of prejudice and personality in Miss Murray's own words. The school-teachers were told that

the field hands of these islands were too low to learn anything, that it was a waste of time to educate or civilize them, that few of them could count their fingers correctly, their language was an unintelligible jargon, and it was impossible to teach them arithmetic.

"The condition of things was appalling," she wrote. "The field hands had been reduced to a state but little above the animals." Many of them had been brought from Africa, smuggled in from ships offshore long after the abolition of the slave trade. She met "a woman who still prayed as her mother had taught her, pouring out water in worship to the full moon, and a tattooed man who told of his wife and children left on 'the other side of the great water.' "

The huts of two rooms had the earth for a floor. An iron pot, a pail, a gourd for a dipper was the furniture, and in these huts, as many people as could well be crowded, slept, wrapped in a blanket for bed and bedclothing. A suit of homespun was furnished once a year to all above ten years of age, and younger ones went unclothed through the summer. Family ties were made and severed at the owner's will. I did not find a girl over sixteen that was not a mother. Morality was unknown. I am not speaking of the house servants or city Negroes but of the field hands on the plantations.

The coming of a school to the island epitomized freedom; the newcomers who brought books seemed like

emissaries sent down by "Maussuh Linkum." We who
have followed those first teachers hear the people tell
of them. Miss Towne was small and slight, but today
they remember her as a large woman and always speak
of her dark eyes full of fire. Miss Murray's perfect de-
votion to her leader is one of the beautiful stories of
the island. Through the heat of the summer, through
discomforts due to a lack of those things we look upon
as sheer necessities, through attacks of fever which
easily discouraged less valiant workers, they carried
on. The Government provided rations, and friends in
the North—Philadelphia, Boston, New York—sent
great cases of clothing. They helped feed and clothe the
people; they nursed them through an epidemic of
smallpox and even had an acquaintance with yellow
fever which followed in the track of the war. They
taught them how to live during those days when an
entire countryside had to work its way up and out
from dependence on others. They were school-teachers
of the whole of life; theirs a mission of love and literacy.

IV

When the war ended, they did not go back North nor
in the trying time of reconstruction; they stayed on
and gave the full measure of their lives. At the end of
forty years their open-handed ministry had become an
island institution. The people still tell how the mis-
tresses of Frogmore always bought everything that
was brought to their door. Blackberries would fill the
kitchen till the cook was in despair. Everyone who
came to the house was first sent to the cook and fed,
which explained what happened to the great plates of

hot biscuits that were brought in for breakfast only to be whisked off so that hotter ones could take their places on the table. Although they engaged a woodcutter by the winter, it was proverbial that these hardworking school-teachers never had a dry stick of wood for their own fires. They thought more of what the work meant to some Negro family than of their own comfort. Perhaps they seemed impractical to some of their critics. But they worked by a carefully thought out plan. Hospitality was one thing; service and pay another; educational values lay in both as they practiced them; but these things at their hands did not lead to begging. Witness this entry, dated May 21, in Miss Towne's diary of 1876, a year the crops had failed: "For the first time in my experience down here I have had people come to the back porch and say (pitifully ashamed too), 'Miss Towne, I hongry.' "

When Miss Towne told her family that she had volunteered for the sea islands, her old nurse bought a gold ring and placed it on her finger, saying, as she looked into those impulsive black eyes which she knew so well, "Patience! Patience! Patience!" The words were inscribed inside the band and we can imagine how often the ring was to be looked at and turned by its wearer in the years that followed.

But there were rich compensations.

Our school does splendidly, though I say it [she wrote on June 7, 1865, soon after the close of the war]. The children have read through a history of the United States and an easy physiology, and they know all the parts of speech, and can make sentences, being told to use a predicate, verb, and adverb, for instance. Ellen's class [Miss Murray's] is writing compositions. We are going to have a grand school exhibition before we close, with dialogues, exercises in mathematics, in grammar, geography, spelling, reading, etc., etc., etc. Our school is a high school already, and we mean to make it more so.

Ten years later, in February, 1875, we find her writing:

I wish you could enjoy the satisfaction of "seeing" the good this money does, as I do. I rejoice more and more daily in the school and its results. St. Helena Island has been peculiarly blessed among "these" Islands even where all have been blessed in comparison with other portions of the South. It is distancing the neighboring islands greatly in thrift, public spirit, and intelligence. One proof of this is the fact that the people "gladly" imposed upon themselves a three mill school tax for this year. There is an ever increasing demand for good schools for the children.

Teacher-making was an important mission of Penn from the first. In the "highest department" of those early days the pupils spent most of their time preparing for the county examinations, as the new public elementary schools for colored children needed instructors and Penn School had to provide them for the islands. "The teachers improve daily," wrote Miss Towne, "and really do better than I had dared to hope. The state needs teachers almost as much as money to pay them, so we must get some ready."

In those years also were started the Island Sunday Schools. The St. Helena Temperance Society was a force for good in more ways than one. A group of the older Negroes formed a Council of Thirty which met after the meeting every Temperance Monday and they began the fight against liquor which is not yet won. Temperance Monday was a picturesque day. All the county schools closed that first Monday in each month, and came to Penn School, prepared to give a "piece" on the program. They were dressed in their best; they marched in as the names of their schools were called. "Eddings Point School" would ring out Miss Murray's voice, "Frogmore," "South Pines," "Old Cuffy," and so through the list of ten county schools, every one of them led by a Penn School graduate. And in a single file the children came, on and on, till Darrah Hall seemed full. In this way a much larger group of island children was brought in touch with the mother school, a step of great value in upbuilding the community.

In the eyes of the parents who had themselves come up from slavery, the free-born boys and girls were especially precious and were pushed forward as fast as possible. From the beginning the pupils came from all parts of the island, from Coffins Point to Land's End, walking, some of them, twelve, fifteen, or even eighteen miles a day, a custom that was kept up more than sixty years.

Our school is a delight [wrote Miss Towne in the late seventies]. It rained last week but through the pelting showers came nearly every blessed child. Some of them walk six miles and back, besides doing their task of cotton picking. Their steady eagerness to learn is just amazing. To be deprived of a lesson is a severe punishment. "I got no reading to-day," or no writing or no sums is cause for bitter tears. This race is going to rise. It is biding its time.

And a decade later, in the eighties, we find the inveterate contagion of her spirit communicating itself to Sarah Orne Jewett who had visited the island one spring, and described it in the "Atlantic Monthly" for August, 1888:

I wish I could have stayed longer to make the sketch better [she wrote Miss Towne] but indeed I wish I could have stayed longer for other and better reasons. The sight of what your faith and patience have wrought on St. Helena's taught me some lessons that I shall never forget.

In the nineties, General Saxton revisited the region.
Back in 1862, as brigadier general of volunteers, he had
been assigned "to take possession of all the plantations
of the South." The cultivation of the land was in his
charge and under his direction the people were organized. When after thirty years of freedom he again
visited St. Helena he was outspoken in saying that the
people did not seem to be the same race. General Saxton saw this registered in the change from the hut on
the slave street to the little whitewashed houses built
on a man's own acres. In those thirty years, stage by
stage, Miss Towne and Miss Murray had seen the home
rise out of the bare earthen floor where the family had
squatted in a circle at mealtime, dipping into the iron
pot with oyster shells for spoons.

The patience, the courage and, withal, the practical
constructive statesmanship of the founders was measured by the great storm of 1893, when a tidal wave
seemed to wipe out in a night the work of thirty years.
The people had secured their land deeds; they had
learned how to win a living out of their holdings, and
they were well on the way to prosperity. A cyclone
from the West Indies drove the tide before it along the
low-lying sea islands like a great sea; homes, stores,
great trees, all went down before it, and the crops were
buried in the mud. People were swept out and lives
were lost. Many saved themselves by floating on roofs,
clinging to the trees, and the deeds of heroism that
night of the howling hurricane proved the morale of
the people. There was no panic, and the men saved their
families or perished with them. No cowardly case of
desertion mars the record. A willing man whose words
you could not understand is on the Penn School farm
today. He has adopted the school and no task is too

menial for him to perform. You might call him queer;
perhaps you would call him half-witted. He was on the
roof of one home that night, and saw all of his family
washed off and disappear. He was a little boy and it
left its mark on him. But he has developed such a love
for the school we wonder how it could be run without
him!

When spring came that year, the men returned to the
fields, and although they were often dizzy for lack of
food, they held on and started again. The land deeds
which they had won by their own labor were not given
up; the islanders stayed on in homes they repaired and
rebuilt; and in a few years all traces of the storm were
gone. But it was remembered by a whole generation,
sung into a spiritual to which the experience gave birth
and recalled by the "basket" names of children born
that terrible year. Some were called "Stormy" in re-
membrance.

Through it all there was no break in the school keeping. The parents were determined that their children
should know books. Throughout the years a demand
for more and better things had been created and stimu-
lated. With education grew a self-respect, reinforcing
the Negroes' natural courtesy. As land and literacy
came to the people, they developed into a law-abiding
community where no magistrate has lived for most of
the time during these nearly seventy years and where
white women have always gone about in perfect safety,
their black neighbors serving as a guard rather than as
a danger.

V

Yet it cannot be said that education of this early type engendered a love for work or encouraged recognition of its basic importance. Laura M. Towne and Ellen Murray were pioneers in their day, and to them must be given the credit for proving that not only the exceptional Negroes, often with admixtures of white blood, would respond to education, but also the manual laborers of the sea-island plantations, the hoers and cotton pickers, whose lot had been that of the biblical hewers of wood and drawers of water since the bootlegging slave ships had left them or their fathers on the coast.

Writes a visitor in 1894:

> We listen to recitations on the theory and practice of teaching, and household hygiene. Some examples in cube root, partnership and discount are rapidly and easily worked, and we inspect beautifully written books, filled with simple bookkeeping.

The scheme of reading, writing, and religion, however, personified by these pioneers of Penn, left great areas of life untouched. Increasingly the object of the school had come to be that of training the teachers for the county schools with their terms of four months. Otherwise the great mass of Negro children, not only on St. Helena but on the adjacent islands would be untouched. The county examinations loomed large. Books were almost the only tools used and the many lessons to be learned through things were left out of consideration.

Books have their limitations. The industrial education that the older generation in slavery had unconsciously absorbed as part of the plantation régime was cut short by the war. The next generation jumped across the furrows their parents had been forced to make straight. Education through the work of the hands very largely stopped. Work under freedom had become nothing more than the drear necessity of making a scant living out of the soil. It lacked the flavor of interest which the school threw about its book learning.

Nor was this peculiar to the race. How many white children in America went through our public schools during these same decades with little consideration of how their education might fit them for the life they must fit into. And all over the world in the mission fields (with noteworthy exceptions), we can see the same tendency—an education that is plastered on, regardless of the life and the needs of the people. To point this out in the case of the early school on St. Helena is not to criticize the old, but to interpret the new.

At one of our first Farmers' Fairs, Moses Dudley, a Penn School graduate, was asked to make a survey of a number of plantations and give a report on the young people who had left the island. His report was brief and to the point. "I might say one third are still in the North; one third come back damaged; one third come back in their coffins, no good to anybody." But we could not wonder that many a young man wanted to leave and seek his fortune elsewhere; in fact we began to wonder why they didn't all go. Farming meant only drudgery and too seldom did they find enough cash in their pockets to carry them through the next year after the hard work in the cotton fields where the whole family worked the season through to raise the crop.

The pattern of New England farm life which, without its diversification, the northern cotton agents had clapped on the one-crop cotton lands while the war was on had not proved a final solution for life and labor on the islands. There were similar limitations to the New England concept of academic education so far as training for life and for larger and better living went. All the more so when confronted with the idea which had gripped a whole generation, that emancipation meant getting away from manual labor.

Penn School started before the creative experiment at Hampton Institute in Virginia. Near the school was a small building put up by the boys under the direction of a carpenter who had learned his trade in the school of slavery. This was the "printing room" and here was the beginning—a bookish beginning to be sure—of industrial education on the island. In a classroom, or out in the grove, a group of girls was taught sewing. The goods sent down from the North after the cyclone were made into garments by the schoolgirls and given to the destitute, and it is recorded of them that they never asked for anything for themselves, so glad were they to be allowed to help in the reconstruction.

Yet the war-time pioneers on this isolated sea island were unconscious of the revolutionary idea which shot out of the active brain of General Armstrong and which, as he developed it at Hampton, was to influence the education of the black child and later the education of the white child as well. Not only was it to influence rural life in the South but educational systems the world over. Out of his experience with Negroes under his command during the war, General Armstrong realized the need of educating the whole personality. This seems like a common idea after its journey for half a century and more through men's minds. Yet in those

post-bellum years it meant a dramatic struggle to break
fresh ground in old fields of thought and educational
habit.

One of the men who began with General Armstrong
and helped him put the idea into deeds, Albert Howe,
told me of a morning in the early days of Hampton
when a whole class "struck." They were to dig a trench
and were started off with shovels and hoes, unfamiliar
tools for a school to put into the hands of its new pupils.
Men, many of them were, who had had military experience, young men who believed in the pot of gold at the
end of the rainbow, whose eyes were far off from the
common tasks in the fields, fixed on a goal to which
algebras and Latin books seemed as stepping-stones.
When they received their direction for the day's work,
they rested on their shovels and began to discuss it
among themselves. Told that they must take the education as given at Hampton if they wanted to stay, they
all sat down by the side of the road, their new educational tools beside them, a rueful crowd in the blue
overalls that seemed so out of keeping as uniforms for
scholars. There they sat till the sun stood at noonday.

When they took up their tools and began to dig,
ground was broken for the new idea in more ways than
one that sunny morning in Virginia. Ground which
meant not only seedtime and harvest crops, but the
flowering out of cultural things once the soil of livelihood had been harrowed.

As the time came when Miss Towne knew she must
lay down her work and that eventually it must be in-
trusted to other hands, she looked beyond the rim of
the islands. She welcomed the suggestion of her niece,
Mrs. William F. Jenks of Philadelphia, to seek advice
from Dr. Hollis B. Frissell of Hampton. She had stayed

at her post till the finish. She had gone through not only the cyclone which swept the islands in the nineties, but its earlier and greater counterpart in the years of reconstruction when the whole economic system of the South was reconditioned, when misunderstandings were inevitable and experiments almost dangerous. Her faith held and she looked forward.

VI

Dr. Frissell has told me how he felt as he was rowed in a bateau across the river from Beaufort. He watched the long sweep of low-lying shore, the marshes glimmering in the lights and the shadows cast by the clouds above. Here on these islands was a distinct section of the Negro people, separated in a measure by the tides and marshes from not a few demoralizing influences of our modern civilization; but reached and influenced none the less by some of the best gifts that the white race had to offer. He took the long drive down the oyster-shell road to Frogmore. In an upper room of the old plantation house where the founder of Penn School, the island physician, the friend of all the people, lay dying, the three missionary educators talked over the future of St. Helena. And Dr. Frissell promised Miss Towne and Miss Murray that their work should not go down.

Some of my readers will remember Dr. Frissell. On his broad shoulders had the Hampton work settled and in his hands it had grown into international proportions. There was room in his imagination, as in the broad South, for Penn and for many another school which turned to Hampton for help and advice. When in the years before his death he came to Penn on his annual visits he always brought with him a sense of peace and the feeling that all was going forward. His marvelous grasp of details gave him the power of becoming as a father to his own students and also to that larger group who turned to him constantly as if they were a very part of Hampton. You remember him with his hand upraised, his great message of "Struggle" on his lips, with his keen sense of humor, which so often set things in their right proportion; with that quiet force—so quiet that you often wondered just where the force lay. As at Hampton, Hollis B. Frissel had become the builder, following Armstrong the founder, so in the rural South and on St. Helena as a part of the rural South, he showed us how to build on foundations that had gone into the very life of the people.

The coming of Dr. Frissell soon led in turn to the coming of a group of young men and women who had been thoroughly inoculated with the Hampton spirit. First, Frances Butler and I, sent out as it were to extend its mission to the very front line. Then Grace Bigelow House came to take the work Miss Butler laid down with her life our first year on the island. Two young Hampton graduates joined us, although we had no dormitories and it meant living in the community and walking to school each morning just as the children walked. When the group increased to five, we had some portable houses sent down and these, put up near our own cottage, became our first teachers' quarters. They weren't very comfortable. Two had to sleep in one tiny room, and there was no general living room. It was not long before the roofs began to leak, but never a word of complaint. Water was carried from a pump in the field, little footpaths ran between our buildings, cockspurs caught us at every step; and until a kind neighbor showed us how to sweep them off with the gray moss that gowns our oak trees, we were in trouble every time we stepped out!

They came down, these young teachers, Virginia-born and Hampton-trained, to hand on what friends had given them in that great school by the sea. "Sugar Lump" was one of these, so called by some of the devoted little children who soon realized, as all St. Helena came to realize, that she had come to give her all. Linnie Lumpkins stood for Hampton in the Fields and no service was too little or too big for her to give to the island people.

At Hampton I had taught many subjects and all grades from preparatories to normal students, and when I came to St. Helena I felt that it had all been a particular Providence that had forced so many new experiences upon me. History seemed to repeat itself at Penn when it seemed wise to give Miss Lumpkins, a skilled primary teacher, the advanced grade and, later, the girls' housekeeping and cooking courses to develop, preparing her for the large work that called her to another part of the state where she would be in the position of an executive, eighteen years later.

Hers was our first school wedding, and then for the first time we used the great yucca blossoms for decorations—beautiful ivory white wedding bells growing on tall stalks, that would make many a city bride envious! She was married to Joshua Enoch Blanton, who had come down to tackle the school farm—an old abandoned cotton field without roads, or fences, or fertile soil. His determination not to give up his first job for five years carried him through many discouragements and for seventeen years he continued the struggle that

prepared him for larger responsibilities as principal of
the Voorhees School. His was a good idea for young
people in school to go out with, if there is the real desire
to serve in their hearts, for the continual jumping about
of teachers in the rural work is one reason for much of
its failure. The "givey-up" feeling has to be battled
with when results seem slow in coming. Rosetta Ma-
son, one of that early group who came "for two years"
and has served the island for twenty-two, James P.
King, with his record of eighteen years, and other
Hampton graduates have proved the value of continu-
ous service. Later, graduates of other schools joined us
in the adventure, and in the circle there is now a group
of islanders, men and women who as boys and girls
trudged the roads from their homes on the farms, who
held on till they won the Penn School certificate, and
some of them, also, a Hampton or Tuskegee or Howard
diploma. They have proved invaluable helpers in the
school, handing on the torch with an understanding of
their own people which did not have to come through
an adaptation to the island.

So the training for leadership of these schools has
been brought to earth, here on our mud flats and down
our oyster-shell roads. Every teacher, whether in classroom, kitchen, shop, or on the farm, carries an equal
responsibility in bringing the more abundant life to the
sea islands.

VII

Newcomers as we were, we were fortunate in soon having a new and modern building to work in and through.
Meanwhile, the little schoolhouse under the live oaks,

The Doctor who dared to inaugurate the practice of medicine on his own island.

rambling and picturesque, historical as being the first one built for the Negroes in the South, had become so timeworn and shaky after some forty years of service that there was nothing to do but to wreck it. It leaked like a sieve. Miss Murray had written of it in one of her later letters:

> I wish our friends could look in upon us during one of our frequent rain storms. The recitation rooms are flooded. One teacher, subject to rheumatic attacks, holds her umbrella over her head as she teaches. In another class the giggling pupils are perched like chickens to roost on the top of the desks, the floor below them being a pool. One teacher thinks it is a good time to scour and has her boys with brooms sweeping out the wet and dirt together.

But what to do with our precious heirloom—the school building of the sixties! The idea and the right moment came. We had found old Aunt Jane living in a house so "ractified" that it was propped up by poles, ready to collapse in the next hard windstorm. "I ain't hab no cyat nor kin on dis island," she had explained as our ponies stopped by her door one day. "My head is berry short ob knowledge, but my mind is on top o' yo'."

That tiny home in the fields haunted us and Aunt Jane with her "mind on top of us" drove us to action. The new schoolhouse had been built and all but the classes in agriculture had been moved over. I had taken those classes of big boys, hoping that by so doing I might be able to popularize the most unpopular of our innovations. Even Miss Murray had felt that the people could get the facts from farm journals and that school time was wasted on that subject. Farming did not connect very well with the ideas on education held on St. Helena Island at the time of our coming. But in one of

those leaky recitation rooms I met the boys and taught
of corn and cotton roots, going with them into the
fields so that they might trace the differences in root
systems in the soil as well as on the painted blackboards. Corn roots and cotton roots became interesting
where only cube roots had held sway for over forty
years. As I faced the boys one especially stormy morning, the plan unfolded itself and I saw the ultimate use
of the schoolhouse which had fairly become a danger
and was no longer really necessary.

Carpentry had already been introduced. These very
boys could take down the old building and use the best
of the boards for a home for Aunt Jane. How could
it be better used? There lay the social content of the
plan for Penn School. And in her own way Miss Murray
was delighted with the plan, too. There in a nutshell,
or, if you will, in the shell of a school, was the epitome
of the new school revolution we were fairly embarked
upon.

These boys liked their new tools. Hitherto they had
always spent their school hours at desks, using only
books for tools till the echoes of industrial education
reached the island from Hampton Institute. The boys,
who had discovered new facts about the corn and the
cotton, those familiar companions of their daily life,
sang as they worked on their new problem—the problem of taking down the old school, and, from the pieces,
constructing a new two-roomed house for Aunt Jane.

The fact that her "ractified" dwelling did collapse
two days after Aunt Jane had moved into their new
house, gave these new social workers great satisfaction. And no less Aunt Jane herself. That morning saw
her down at the school.

I t'aw't I wuz goin' to dead. But de Lord, he put me in dat house dis day. All dem young boys dey say, "Aunt Jane, I help on yo' house," an' dem chillun hab good mannus. I neber know one of dem gib me no back answer yit. I wuz mo' dan glad. I wuz glad till I could be glad no mo'. My time ain't come yit, yo' see! Quick as dey tek me out ob dat ole house, hit fall! God is a feelin' God! He feels! He wuz jis waitin' to git help! I'se so tanksful [she sighed] I'se so tanksful I cyan' 'spress muhself. But I tells de Lord.

When her little house was "christened," an island custom which means a service of blessing the new home, Aunt Jane had a pumpkin ready for us to carry home, a fit gift to express her thanksgiving, golden fruit from her own field.

It was significant that the historic schoolhouse should end in a home for one of the old people. The founders had built their work on the homes of the people, and largely through their efforts had the people learned the value of the deeds to their farms. Their successors had come with the hope of connecting those homes and farms so closely with the school that those land deeds might remain in the hands of the people.

For back of the changes in educational methods we had gone to the island to introduce, lay a great economic fact. Here were hundreds of acres. Here were hundreds of homes. The acres and the homes were theirs, to have and to hold if they could keep abreast of the times, if they could dig the wealth in their own farms. And here were hundreds of children getting book learning but not getting their roots down into the soil, the very basis of life. Could our old Liberty Bell help ring in a new freedom—help wake up the oncoming boys and girls to see that the responsibility for holding what their grandfathers and grandmothers had handed down to them rested on their own shoulders? Would it be possible for Penn School to help develop a rural life rich enough to hold the generation that had not won the acres by their own labor?

PART II

HOW WE BROUGHT THE FARMS TO SCHOOL

I

T was a bright but cold day, twenty-five February ago, that I first saw Penn School. We had lingered over our breakfast at Frogmore, the plantation house which had been the home of its Founders since those war-time days when school-teaching was first started among the island people. We had delighted in the comfortable beginning to our day, Josephus appearing first in his overalls to build the fires in the great fireplaces and later in his spotless white coat to bring in hot cakes from the kitchen across the yard. And around eleven o'clock we finally started down the road in an ancient buggy which was drawn by a cream-colored horse with the name of "Pleasant." Surely his lines had fallen in pleasant places for rarely was he enticed off the walk, his mistress feeling that the use of a whip was wicked in itself, and a bad object lesson to the people.

For forty years and over, a devoted track had been beaten between Frogmore and Penn School. Along the road we overtook boys and girls meandering in the same direction, all neatly dressed, for clothes have had a large part to play in the educational processes of this race who love color and beauty. Best clothes for school and church had been the rule on St. Helena.

We rejoiced in the bright colors as we drove the three miles to the little rambling schoolhouse that had so long been the center of the revolution that had added learning to liberty for the bondspeople of these great isolated plantations, who had raised the famous sea-island cotton and who seldom, in slavery days had come in contact with their owners or with any form of white civilization. The setting of the old plantation life unfolded before us. The dull browns of last year's cotton stalks brought into relief the vivid greens of the oaks and the pines. We came to a great meadow of marsh grass, with a little tidal river winding its way through; our sandy roàd became a white oyster-shell causeway for a short distance; and lights and shadows played across the golden browns of the marsh. There was the occasional flash of a Kentucky cardinal and we heard the songs of many mocking birds. Even in February the white wild plum blossoms along the roadside made the chill air seem a contradiction, and brilliant sunshine made me forget the cold until we went into Darrah Hall to which the school bell was summoning the children.

Here we sat and shivered! Never did I feel colder even in the snows of Dutchess County in our New York winters for here it seemed to be concentrated, intensified. About a hundred children faced us as we sat on the platform. The Hall was built to seat a thousand, and empty spaces stretched behind them. Even so, when the group of boys and girls, none of them clad warmly enough to sit in the cold, began to sing, we could forget our own shivering and theirs and listen to the harmonies of,

> Gib me dat ole time religion
> Gib me dat ole time religion
> Gib me dat ole time religion
> It is good enough fo' me.
>
> It is good w'en you're in trouble
> It is good w'en de doctor gib yo' obuh

and so on, verse after verse, till I found it impossible not to join. We all sang ourselves warm that morning.

Late comers began to drift in and took their seats facing the open door instead of the platform; a simple

matter for the benches had no backs. That was the
penalty for being late; a rather joyous penalty, I
thought, for who would not rather look into the great
oak trees than face the bleak walls? Before the chapel
service was over there were almost as many children
facing backward as forward, and the empty seats between the two groups divided the "sheep" from the
"goats." Next we followed the long line of "scholars"
as they marched single file from Darrah Hall and scattered themselves among the various rooms of the old
schoolhouse of the sixties—the ultimate fate of which
I have already told you. There had never been any
money to spend on plaster, but the rough boards had
been painted a charming blue in some of the rooms, a
perfect background for dark faces. Spaces painted
black served as blackboards; a few old maps; a globe
in Miss Murray's room; rough desks made to seat two
but often holding four; some book cupboards, and that
was all! But no, I've forgotten to speak of the stoves—
an iron box stove in one corner of each room—and
work began that morning in each room with a general
stove stoking.

While the classes were getting ready for the day's
work, which included the usual school motions as well
as the fireworks, I saw Miss Murray quietly turn back
the hands of the little clock so the school should seem
to begin at its regular hour of eleven o'clock in the
morning instead of the actual opening that cold day—
after twelve. "It makes no difference to the scholars,"
she said, with her eyes twinkling, and I knew why a
little later when I discovered that there were so few
clocks in the homes that the sun had to serve as timekeeper!

Visiting the classes, I was amazed by feats of

memory. Pages of history were recited with hardly a
word changed; long lines of presidents and dynasties
could be given, dates included, without hesitation. The
blackboards were covered with examples in cube root
and algebra; a group of the most advanced pupils were
deep in Latin prose. Later we heard a class recite in
physics though the little schoolhouse could boast of
no laboratory. In the geography class they identified
the wiggly black lines on the map as water courses, but
these had nothing to do with the blue and shining tide
rivers that some of the boys and girls had crossed in
coming to school. States and their capitals were as
glibly recited as the kings and queens, and a bit of
humor was added when I learned that "George Washington is de capital ob dese United States."

Some of the older boys must have learned something
of the fashioning of the books which played so large a
part in their school life. A small press was used by Miss
Murray to print sheets containing the historical facts
necessary for those who would try the county examinations every spring and autumn. Yet, in themselves,
these printed sheets symbolized for me the old method
of education—isolated facts learned not because they
fitted into life but because they fitted into the examinations!

The year's work culminated in an annual exhibition.
Darrah Hall would be crowded with the parents breath-
lessly watching the feats performed by their offspring.
On one such day the boys and girls in the history class
were dressed as the kings and queens they recited
about, and to the people and to the pupils it was a
spectacle never to be forgotten. To show that they
really knew the long line of England's royalty, they
were asked to recite backward and beginning in the

middle as well as forward. Every child in school was exhibited on that well-named day, and all the classes gave a recitation of some sort, every question and answer thoroughly memorized.

II

As we who had come from Hampton studied the old school and faced its problems—human problems they were—our first concern was how to adapt to a day school the methods of vocational education we had learned in a large boarding institution.

Most training schools for Negroes are boarding schools. Here on the island the new leadership must be applied to the difficulties, the needs, the opportunities of a community. The whole island was our dormitory; and in time the whole island was to become our school. The children return to their homes each evening and connect those homes with the school with an unbroken intimacy. The mass of children in a thousand communities in the South cannot go to boarding schools. The rural teacher must be interested in the family as well as in the child and the larger community interests are as important as the classrooms.

So our first step in reorganizing the work was to get out into the community, and in contrast to the plodding "Pleasant" who so calmly drew the buggy from Frogmore, Miss House and I boldly mounted the school horses (neither one of us ever having ridden before) and that first year began "slashin' about de island." "Dat big hawss is a vain t'ing fo' safety," old Mrs. Juno would often remind us, but we found our saddles the best means for reaching the many homes up and down the oyster-shell roads, and beyond them on the long grass-grown lanes through which the children came.

The horses that have carried us deserve to rank as community workers! First came Community Maud and then Jubilee, Welcome, Come-again, Wonder, Wander, Sunshine, and now Community Joy. One of my greatest failures was met when I tried to add horse-buying as a side line to my school-teaching job. I was to learn the trickery of a horse dealer, for the apparently lively horse I selected in Savannah, thinking that he deserved the name of Jubilee, discarded his city sprightliness during his week on trial like any Dr. Jekyll and Mr. Hyde in the horse line. A wiser school-teacher decided once for all to keep hands off the stock question, even if it did seem an economy to combine all sorts of school shopping in one trip to the city. The real Jubilee, selected later, spent the rest of her life on our roads.

Our ponies carried us over the island. We learned to know the people and they began to understand us "foreigners" better. When the mother of six Penn School children said, "Yo' ain't foot my floor dis year," she expressed a really keen regret; and when another said, "I'm glad to welcome de intelligence ob Penn School this day," we felt spurred on to get about faster. The ponies began to be noticed.

"Yo' done git dat hawss up where yo' come f'om," declared a man we met on the road.

"No, indeed," I answered, "we bought this pony at Land's End."

"Den yo' done mek him grow t'ru de mout," he exclaimed. Remembering the rough little creature we had brought in a few months before, we could see how the boys were spreading their lessons in animal indus-

try out over the farms. These equine community
workers really ushered in the school revolution for they
showed the trotting Miss Ichabods the conditions on
the farms and in the homes and the need for linking
them up to the school. As I shall tell you in a later chapter, that work is now carried on by four regular exten-
sion workers of Penn School, and the classroom teachers themselves are out in the fields for a part of their
regular schooltime.

"Dese teachers are here to lif' our boys and girls upstairs. Too many fall on their way up. Not all reach
upstairs, and I am one myself who slip, so now I cyan'
'spress myself as I wish," said one of our young fathers. "Too many fall on their way up!"—that is the
problem in all our rural work. In 1904, when our work
on the island was still measured in months, I risked
Ruskin who said, "I have always found that the less we
speak of our intentions the more chance there is of our
realizing them." Instead we began to publish as widely
as possible the new plans for Penn, plans which were
to make this school a community center, plans which
called for a school farm, for adequate buildings and
trained teachers.

For forty years Penn School graduates had stood by
the school and had given back to the younger group all
that had been given to them. To replace them with
teachers with a larger training and outlook was a necessity and the most difficult operation that had to be
performed in all the transformation.

The building of a modern schoolhouse to replace the
old one marked the change in more ways than size or
newness. Here was our lever in introducing the idea of
industrial education. That the new building cost money
was plain to the whole island, and could be used to

teach that education cost money! The little crossroads
public schools, maintained out of taxation by the
county, ran but four or five months a year. The people
had been asked to pay the whole of ten cents a year
for the larger chance each child had at Penn when at
last the Founders had been compelled to ask their help
in supporting the school. When we arrived the annual
fee had been raised to one dollar. It was a principle
with Miss Murray that every child should have a free
education as his due. It needed time and patience to
convince her that the time had come to raise the fee
to five dollars at one stroke! The people were more
easily convinced, though I heard one mother call it a
"very expensionate school." A parent would come saying that Ezekiel was "wut de five dollars, but Benola's
haid too t'ick," and it looked as if an unfair division of
opportunity were coming to the children. Right here
we drove in our wedge. That parent would be told that
he could pay the one dollar and that Benola could work
out the other four. The problem of finding hard cash in
a community which seldom handled money and so
largely was caught in the crop-loan, store-credit
economy of the South, opened the door to hundreds of
island children in this way instead of closing it. This
was an unexpected by-product of building the new
schoolhouse. The worth of the school was to be measured in fees. I think the children liked it from the beginning. It was a lot more fun for them to work in a
group that was not confined to brothers and sisters; to
have the leadership in work of a teacher instead of a
parent was a novel change. It soon became the custom
for all the children to work out the four dollars. Farm
tools and scrubbing brushes for the first time took their
proper place beside the books. This step made it easier

to weave in industrial education as a part of the regular schedule a little later.

III

Still the children came in their best clothes and it was a common sight to see boys working in their jackets with the sweat pouring off their faces. The fight for overalls and work dresses is not fully won yet; but we can't expect to accomplish everything in one generation. Clothes had been of the texture of freedom. "Come out ob dat fiel'! Yo'll injure yo' shoes!" was a call of distress from more than one parent; and a day school should meet the problem by providing dressing rooms and lockers. They came to school often weary before school tasks could begin, boys and girls walking from one to nine miles, and in time our school has met that problem too, by providing trucks, called "chariots," which are sent to certain rallying points to shorten the too-long walks. These trucks take the place of dormitories in a measure and the children continue to be the rural newspapers as they carry the news from school to home every evening. Progress may be slower in individual cases than if the pupils were housed at the school, but we believe the need of the whole community is better met, more fundamentally helped by this process.

"Hey! yo' better hol' up yo' haid an' look at de sun an tell me whut time he is," explains another of our chief difficulties and one of our first goals. The sun is a poor timekeeper on cloudy days! The shriek of the oyster factory whistle, or that of the cotton gin; the school bells rung at intervals; ebb tide, flood tide,

young flood, day-clean, or when "de fust star shine"—
all served the community, but time was of small importance as it was so shifting a thing. On rainy days
there was no school. On gray days the late pupils far
outnumbered the punctual ones. We had turned them
about in Darrah Hall so they all faced the platform and
some had learned more about time in earning that
school fee; but there was always an uncertainty about
our finding pupils in their seats in the morning.

When we set out to break the island tradition that
country children "had to be tardy," we started the reform with great solemnity. The school was called together just before the children set out for home. The
unusualness of the time had its effect; they felt the air
charged with something momentous. We gave them
the figures of the week before. We showed them how
much time had been actually lost for a week, and if
continued what it meant—for a month, for a year. We
made a clear picture of their very crooked road to learning. And then we told them they could be late once a
week. I think that seemed like a sort of gift to them.
In fact we gave them five days a month, but after that
they were to turn themselves out of school if they
didn't "catch the line" as it entered Darrah Hall. We
wondered that night what would be the outcome; we
hoped that eventually it would lead to clocks in the
homes.

Next morning we had a breath-taking experience. All
the children came on time except one little girl who
crept to the office for her "excuse"; in a week the "excuse line" was reduced from sixty and over, to six! But
the test to the principals and teachers came when the
children began to forget the solemnity of that first
school meeting, and they had to turn back after the

long walks, often because their parents had exacted too long a home task before they started.

However, the reform, drastic as it seemed, was the turning point for a whole generation with respect to promptness. The opening of school was gradually moved up from eleven o'clock to ten and finally to nine-thirty. Chapel service also was changed to the noon hour so that workers on the farm could come in with less interruption—a definite step in the adjustment of school to farm.

Raising the fee had given new dignity to the school; requiring that the pupils report on time was the second step and the third might be called getting the books out of the schoolhouse where they had been walled up so long. After all, the Penn books had been comparatively few in number and they had been held to be too precious to be trusted in the hands of the pupils. We began with one book apiece for each grade, to be paid for by the child. The children loved the idea and the parents found it quite possible to take this next step. Today every child owns the usual quota of schoolbooks and so proud are they of these possessions that they are determined to carry them home every night. Whether they live a mile or six you will meet the boys and girls with their loads of books, the hall mark of Penn School children! The teachers have had to regulate this for the sake of their health, but we let the step take its own gait for a year or two.

The owning of books has, of course, opened the doors of the school library wider. All grades are given a "library hour" when they spend the time in the library with their teacher to show them how to use it. This has increased the demand and now books go to hundreds of homes. Our librarian wrote to me one time when I was "on the road" for funds to keep the school open:

You will be interested to hear that one hundred and ten books have been taken out from the library this month, and it is only the 17th. But I have such a hard time with the younger children! There are only about ten books in the library that they can read and when twenty or thirty come in at one time, I am simply swamped. Yesterday all the little girls and all the little boys of Grade II came in and each was set on getting a book. One little girl threw herself at the bookshelves with passionate zeal, crying, "I'se gwine git me a book dis day!" and the things she did to my neatly arranged shelves were a caution. But there simply weren't any books her size to "git." I felt like an impostor. Little Martin Washington, after searching about for a minute, came to my side and announced in a very resigned tone, "Cyan' fin' no book, muh." I gave him one that I knew he couldn't read, thinking he could look at the pictures, but presently back he came, "Don' want dis book, muh." I took it back and told him I was very sorry, but as there weren't any books he did want—to run away and I'd try to get one for him next week. Presently I looked around and there he was once more—"Cyan' fin' no book, muh." I told him again all I had told him before and more also, and I thought he was convinced, but after all the other children had gone back he came and remarked, still without heat, "Cyan' fin' no book, muh."

How we wish that primers and readers and nature books, well illustrated and with good print, would rain down on St. Helena! I have in mind not only the families of the Penn School children but we send a library box, made by the boys in the school shop, with leather hinges and provided with a padlock, large enough to hold about thirty books, to each of the little county schools on St. Helena and on two or three near-by islands—schools that struggle with a four to six months' term and a most meager equipment.

IV

The civilization of any people can be measured by the books in the homes; but the distribution of books and what they stand for, out from the school, was the lesser of the two currents we endeavored to set in motion. Our object was to bring the island life itself into the classrooms—into the little world of teaching that had been altogether too much bound up in printed words. Mine was a very stiff class that marched out to the woodpile one morning twenty-five years ago to measure a cord instead of learning about it on a page in the arithmetic; a much surprised class that paced off an acre of land in the next field, instead of sitting at their desks and "doing" some problem in the books as to carpet measurement, when there was not a carpet in the home, nor a yard of it in the store. But these boys and girls gradually began to like the change from books and memory to the world about them.

Realities began to crop out in the classrooms. Some youngsters were being shown the secrets of subtraction. Said the teacher, "If I send you to the store with seven cents and tell you to get one pound of sugar which costs seven cents, what will you have left?" "One pound of sugar, muh," promptly answered a little beginner. In another class I found that the children had been sent on an imaginary trip to the store with two dollars to spend. Among the things they were to buy was ten cents worth of candy. When the answer was called for, all the children but one had sixty-five cents change. The odd child had seventy cents. Asked to explain, he said, "I cyan' eat mo' dan five cents wut ob candy." Nature study early became popular. When one

teacher discovered that her grade had never seen the
fascinating transformation of tadpoles to frogs, she
started some eggs off in a washbowl in her classroom.
This became the most thrilling corner in the school.
All ages achieved an early arrival to see what had happened in the night. One of the old fathers, drawn to
that corner by the strange tales his children told him,
came to my office on his way home saying: "Dese teachers sho' teach we a heap ob ting. I ben lib yuh all my
life an' huccome I ain't know pollywog tu'n to frog?"

For about four years the old and the new went on together, and what a school of contrasts we were! In one
room all the youngsters would be learning their lessons
aloud in the old way, the singsong suggesting a school
in the Orient. In another room a class would be learning pages and pages by rote, and then would come
through the hall a new teacher with her class to measure that hall or to go to the sandpile for geography or
even to the field or garden for real agriculture that belonged in no book. Yet it was no easy matter to in-
corporate agriculture, upon which the whole life of the
islands depends, in our scheme of education. The people
had always farmed and the new Hampton-trained
teachers were looked upon with suspicion, our school
farmer as "a mere boy."

"Various branches hang on de wings ob dis school,"
said one of the parents who had caught the new spirit.
What in fact were the main branches which registered
our new growth out from the sturdy stem of the School
of the Founders? First came the school farm and then
the school shops. We saw that the school must be built
up out of its own farm land if it were to teach the
islanders things of fundamental value for a new time.
Yet when we began, this school on its old plantation

site had no garden and we ate canned vegetables all of
that first winter; it had no poultry plant nor turkey
roost. Abandoned cotton fields surrounded us and the
only crop those fields produced were cockspurs which
made us miserable when we walked out. "Where is the
farm?" innocently asked our first visitor who was ex-
pecting to see an agricultural school!

But slowly this branch of the work began to leaf.
Those cotton fields that had produced nothing but cotton since "before the war," and each year less of it,
began to grow cowpeas and corn; rotation of crops became a school slogan. Thanks to Miss Murray's native
patriotism all the older pupils knew the English kings
and queens and the English Magna Charta, a copy of
which hung in the hall, but it must now be borne in
upon them that their own Magna Charta was to come
to them through the knowledge and the practice of
rotation of crops. It was learned as to meaning and as
to spelling but it was not known and understood till we
started our "miniature farm" near the schoolhouse.
Rotation had been first practiced on the school farm,
and land that had produced eight and ten bushels of
corn to the acre began to yield from twenty to thirty.
But the school farm itself was too big to "see," and so
one acre, located near the road was measured off by
the children and divided into thirds, one grade planting
cotton, another sweet potatoes, another corn. Careful
accounts were kept and a winter crop of oats and vetch
followed. The groups kept up this crop rotation for
three years so all could visualize on that acre as on a
map; and arithmetic and agriculture played into each
other's hands. We thank Clemson, South Carolina's
State Agricultural College, for this idea; and the little
play we wrote to dramatize it, called "The Soil Builders

and the Soil Robbers," was printed by the college and distributed to other schools in the state.

Our first agricultural lessons had been based on school gardens like those of any city school in the North. Each pupil was given a small plot to cultivate. Perhaps it was a good way to begin, for as it was so absurdly different from the home work it caught their interest; but we began that way because we did not know any better. Very soon we discovered that it was not the right way to continue. The small gardens were only play and would have lost their interest. Just before this happened, we put a whole group out on another school acre of old cotton land to raise corn according to the demonstration method. Here was the real thing. Again arithmetic, for the acre was measured by the children; the land rented from the school; and the cost of the seeds, fertilizer, time of "man and mule," and the net returns of the crop made a computation worth while. When the children saw the actual money the crop had made—for of course the school bought the fruits of their labor—they had the fun of choosing what the amount would buy for their classroom. New enthusiasm was thus kindled for next year's work.

One of our best records on a school acre was that of St. John School, our little ungraded school on the grounds which has been the practice school for our teachers-to-be and which has given us some of the problems of the ungraded county schools to work on. Their teacher had belonged to my first agriculture class at Penn, which lost and broke some of their tools that first year, thinking that if the tools disappeared, agriculture would leave the school. His hatred of the subject had turned into love—an evangel of husbandry. Whenever he sent out the call in the summer that their

acre of corn needed the children (in those days we had
no summer term) there was no lack of response. True
agriculturist that he was, he had planted watermelons
around the corn rows, so the work was turned into a
feast worth walking miles for in the hot sun.

It was a natural step, a few years later, to transfer the
corn acre work for the older groups at the school to
home acres on the island farms, and there it has stayed
as the home farms have become more and more a part
of the school equipment. Their development belongs to
another chapter, but we had come to see that if the education we were to give at Penn were to mean to fit for
living, the school farm and the home acres had to become classrooms.

V

We had cause for thanksgiving that the school held its
own during these years of transition and seemed to be
growing stronger. Probably this was due to the fact
that the children themselves loved it, and, won for the
new ways, proved strong enough to stand up against
the doubting Thomases in their own households. Or,
perhaps, it was because the new schoolhouse with its
brightness and comfort could be a compensation for
the new education that went with it and seemed so
wasteful of time to the people to whom only books
heretofore had stood as the proper tools for education.

Moreover, we were unwelcome prophets in predict-
ing the advent of the boll weevil, long in advance of
its coming to the islands; but a situation was surely at
hand when the long-staple cotton crop of the sea islands
could no longer be depended upon as the only means

of support. A farming system of over sixty years had to be questioned and a new economy begun. It is no wonder the school was under suspicion for not only were we bringing new methods of teaching, not only were we eliminating some of the "higher" studies like algebra and Latin, but we were taking a very questionable stand in agriculture, the one thing that was understood by the islanders as their own field in more ways than one. It was a relief—and at the same time a difficult reputation to live up to—when we heard one of the ministers pray for the school "which is the light, it is the bridge over the Red Sea into the promised land for we people, it is the Moses and it is the pillar of cloud by day and the pillar of fire by night."

As the school farm took form, food crops were emphasized. We had been buying canned beets and corn, we had been waiting for our milk to be brought in each morning from a nearby plantation and every breakfast was an uncertainty. A boy used to appear, riding an ox by our windows, for in the beginning there were no roads on the school farm, and as often as not he appeared at ten o'clock as at seven when he was expected. One morning we sent Matilda out for the milk and when she returned after we had long finished our simple breakfast, I asked her, "Did you wait for the cow to be milked?" and she answered, "Yes, muh."

Better farm animals helped on the revolution. Mary, Martha, Thanksgiving, and Victory were the mules who led the advance. Chickens and pigs were added and a small herd of cattle built up from grades with the pure-bred bull one of the trustees sent down to the school. Even the dogs were not forgotten and our beautiful black collie, Constantine, son of St. Helena, was as well known on the island as the ponies.

One day an abbreviated dog show held the school spellbound and if we did not have circus bleachers we had the same effect, for boys and girls in the back rows stood on the benches to see the performance. Speaking first to the point that a dog well bred and well trained was worth owning, explaining what "well-bred" and "pure-bred" meant, I called on Con himself to show the meaning of a well-trained dog. Speaking in my usual conversational tone, I asked him to say "Good morning," to lie down, to die for his country like a good soldier, to catch the bit of cracker on his nose, the audience growing more and more delighted as he went through his repertoire without a miss. But the interest increased when I sent him to say "Good morning" to others on the platform, the dog picking out the right person by the process of elimination. The height was reached when I told him to go and find "Grace," the only name he knew for Miss House, who in the meantime had hidden behind the movable blackboard. Under the piano he looked, out of the window, down the aisles, and, finally, as he started to go to the open door, he caught the scent and the show ended amid applause from the benches and wild barking at his own victory. Some of the island homes begin to boast of better pups and a generation is springing up to appreciate dog stock. A rural school has as many sides to it as an automobile factory.

Our fields began to change as agriculture settled into the curriculum. The boys marched out to clear new land on the school farm that had not seen a crop since the tasks of overseers had kept their grandfathers on those acres. They cut through the thick tangle of growth in advance of Victory and Thanksgiving; plow points were broken as men and mules turned the soil.

Using big tools has a charm for any well-developed country boy. It was when some rather large stumps had to be dug up by sheer muscle that the first group came in, saying that they were "sick in the side." A night's rest and an assurance that they could do a man's job resulted in their return and that was the last of the complaints against the new work. But the beautiful field that has the record of fifty-three bushels of corn and 453½ bushels of sweet potatoes to the acre, still goes by the name of "The Sticks."

Our next move was to carve out seven acres of our best land on "The Sticks" for a study farm. The block was measured off by the agriculture boys and put into crops that an island farm should carry—crops for food for the home and stock, crops for cash—and for land improvement. Here all the classes have had work during their agriculture periods, following expenditures as well as receipts, and giving an opportunity to our senior boys to serve as supervisors in the group. This put into practice again the principle of our "miniature" farm, but on a larger scale. It opened the way for school agriculture in the field graded as carefully as the classroom subjects are graded. And this grading will be true of all our program of industrial studies, built around the basic nurture of the soil.

VI

A decadence in all handwork on the island had been an unforeseen by-product of emancipation. The strict requirements of the plantation régime had been removed; the freed man, as we have seen, longed for the book to take the place of all labor, and in the course of

half a century, it had come to pass that practically all
the farm repair work was carried to Beaufort, our nearest town on Port Royal Island, or perhaps to Savannah.
When soon after my arrival I heard a white friend say
of the island boys that he never saw such a total lack
of mechanical skill, that nearly all who attempted to
unscrew a nut naturally turned it to the right, I wondered why they shouldn't; for they never had an opportunity at home or at school to loosen nuts or struggle with any mechanical appliances except the tiny
plows and cultivators which no one taught them to
keep in order. If the farms were to come to school,
surely the farm tools and home necessities should have
a place in the school curriculum. And so the school
shops became another main limb for the "various
branches" which "hang on de wings ob dis school."

Our Cope Industrial Building was the first large
structure built by the islanders themselves—built to
celebrate the fiftieth anniversary of the founding of
Penn School. Under Hampton graduates they worked,
the walls of oyster-shell concrete rising to song and
laughter. It was a normal development, using their
own steer carts to carry sand and oyster shells, the
sand brought to the school landing on the school's boat
from nearby rivers, the oyster shells from nearby
oyster factories. And so island resources, muscles, and
spirit were utilized and "We Building" took its place
in the school's equipment to make possible a larger
service to the island.

Into the new industrial building went first of all a
class of boys who were learning to "sew" the island
baskets. This bit of industrial work is not only a hang-
over from the old days but has an African origin. We
had found Alfred Graham, one of the plantation crafts-

men who had held on to his gift, using rushes that grow in the tide rivers, and sewing them with strips of palmetto. He was an old man, very straight and self-respecting. Often he would come into my office "to git de light on hit" so that he could serve as an interpreter to his people when the new doings at Penn needed so much the native bridge. His loyalty never wavered when our doings were most revolutionary.

He had learned to make baskets from his African uncle and in turn passed his skill on to his grand-nephew. From the first work baskets the shop has taught the boys of today to make scrap baskets needed in every home, clothes hampers which are sometimes beautiful enough for a museum (these were developed from the old cotton baskets), and wood baskets such as we found used on the farms. These last are oval and if "lined with pitch within and without" could have served to conceal the infant Moses in the bulrushes.

The grand-nephew who now teaches the craft has been through the temptations his boys have to meet. Within a year of his graduation he had drifted to a nearby city where the lights and cash and good times proved to be more alluring than the country school. But his adopted mother had other plans for George. She followed him "off island," and her determination resulted in the boy developing into a graduate teacher at Penn with all the feeling for the beautiful craft and all the pride of his old African ancestors in its standard being maintained.

From all corners of the island came the farm tools to be mended at the new Cope shops, often the boy who mended the tool taking it home at night. Down the oyster-shell road anew went closer connections between school and farm and home. Not only did the

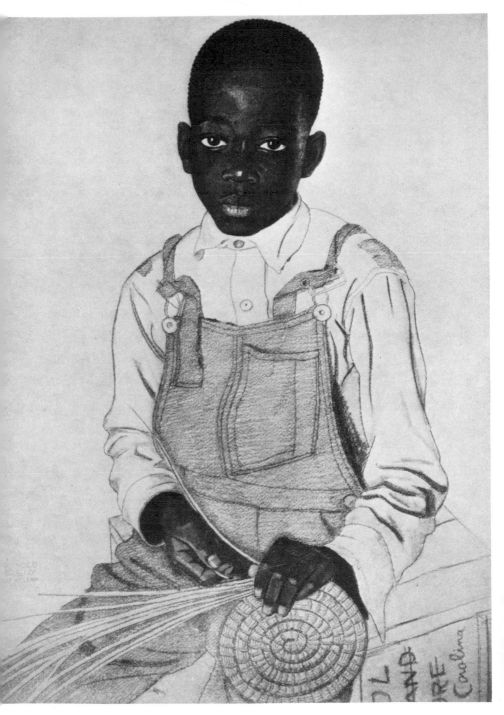

Learning to make an island basket.

blacksmith and wheelwright shops mend the tools; the carpenter shop took its important place in the scheme of life. Proudly wrote one of the boys:

> My industrial work is carpentry. This is the first year that I ever took carpentry. Ever since I began taking industrial work I was taking cobbling. I like carpentry but I like cobbling better. I know it, and you know it too, when a man gets on a fourteen or fifteen story building his life is in danger. I have never seen a man on a fifteen story building, but if life spare me I am hoping to see one, or I might gets on one. I think cobbling is the most comfortable trade.

The young carpenters have thought less of sky-scrapers than of better homes for the island and have shared in building them. The young cobblers and harness makers have been repairing shoes to keep hundreds of children in school. They have seen the transformation from crude leather straps mended with strings to the best grade of harness. The young blacksmiths and mechanics have seen automobiles come, not only to the school but also to some of the island homes; the Cope shop is their repair shop and service station and many an island boy and girl now turns the nut in the right direction as naturally as a white brother.

All of the work in all these shops has been teaching the real things of life. Tools have joined the pens and pencils of the classroom. The young farmers have moved up from the primitive hoe to the mowing machine, the rice thresher, the tractor. They are learning how electricity is made through the school's plant, how to run the water engine, how to run an incubator, how to make cane syrup. The kitchen range and the sewing machines, the canner and garden tools, good laundry tubs and clothes boilers have come to the hands of their sisters. For lessons in housekeeping in all its branches, in sewing and nursing, have given them an equivalent background of reality.

We have only a small dormitory, which is, however, of importance in giving the home side and the home problems to the school within itself. We began with three boys. One was Jacob, another Solomon, and the third broke the biblical succession and bore the name Richard. In those early days, I remember a boy coming in with his clothes tied up in a calico square; bright colored it was, and the school was a metropolis to that boy. We try to have all the graduates spend two or three years on the school farm. The milkers and the girl cooks, who get up at four-thirty in the dark of winter, make a striking contrast to those boys and girls who used to wander in for an eleven o'clock opening of the older school. There is a fine struggle on the part of many of the parents to keep these children in school, and standards have risen. Witness the trunks and suitcases which have taken the place of the calico squares.

VII

As we look back over our years of struggle to add to the classroom work at Penn those things that would teach the larger life we have come to see the necessity for changing some of our plans. A school in a community needs to be elastic if it is to keep growing.

In the days of our beginnings, the hands of the older folk went up in dismay when they realized that we had come to bring work into the school which did not come directly from the books. We had to make the first steps fit very closely into the actual needs of the moment. Industrial education had to begin with an

actual money value if it were to begin at all. The school
fee had been raised and the boys and girls were allowed to "work it out." The parents liked it for it saved
them five dollars in cash per child, and the children
liked it for they enjoyed the novelty of working at the
school in the larger groups. Larger brothers and sisters
would work out the fee for the younger ones in school
and altogether the move was a popular one. But there
were dangers in it and two years ago we decided the
plan must go.

The dangers lay in the fact that pupils and parents
began to think that all work done on the farm and in
the shops was of money value to the school, forgetting
or never realizing that the farm was for the boys, and
not the boys for the farm; that the shops, kitchens,
sewing room, gardens, and dormitories on the school
farm were for the pupils as truly to be used as educational tools as the books and blackboards in the classrooms. This was an entirely natural result of the plan
of work. And it had its dangers for the teachers as well.
So long as there was a cash value placed on the work
per hour, the tendency was to let the pupils who did
the best work stay on a job after they had learned it.
And so it could happen that they might reach the end of
their schooling and miss some of the branches on the
wings of learning. Isaiah graduated before he reached
the poultry plant!

We now called for the school fees in cash. By this
time work at the school had become so much a part of
the island experience that the change could be made
easily.

We do not pay your children for studying their arithmetic
[we said] so why should we pay them for studying agriculture in the fields or carpentry in the shop, or cooking in the

kitchen? All the men and women in these departments are teachers and rank with the classroom teachers.

The whole community saw the point and the change was made!

But this change in the fee system was just one step in bringing our industrial work to the rank of our academic work. It must be kept clearly in mind that Penn School is not a trade school nor merely an agricultural school. The farm and the shops and all of the practical work are to play their part in equipping the boys and girls for life in the country with ideas of leadership in home making, farming, teaching. Those who go "off island" are the better prepared to meet the realities of life if they have been meeting them all through their school course. All practical work can be educational in the life of school children if the aim of that work and not just the work itself is kept in the minds of the children, parents, and teachers.

I shall tell in the next chapter how our school year has been dovetailed into the island seasons. We have our spring, summer, winter, and autumn terms, and counting out the vacation periods, these terms are each about ten weeks in length. Four of the most important dates in our school year are our assignment meeting days. Let me describe a meeting of the agricultural and industrial teachers who come together on the Thursday before the first Monday in each term. They are all men, these teachers, with experience in the shops and farm departments going back for several years. Each brings the records made by the boys in his department. Perhaps another Isaiah is the boy under consideration. He has spent the autumn term in the carpentry shop. He has done only fairly well; he cannot be called "dependable," but he is waking up. The question is: Shall

Isaiah be assigned again to that same department, or to
another? And then comes discussion. The teachers see
Isaiah in various lights. He is discussed as a boy, and
not as a carpenter. He may be assigned to the same
shop, the men deciding that he is on the verge of making good, and another term there will mean more than
if his work is changed. On the other hand they may feel
that he is more likely to make good if he leaves that
work to return to it at a later time, when he will begin
where he left off, but with a greater ambition to be
promoted to the next higher group.

This brings us to our new system of grading the industrial work, and to visualize that I must tell you
about our groups. Formerly the pupils worked according to their grades in the classrooms. There are serious
objections to such a rule-of-thumb method when you
are dealing with the realities of industrial work. Some
boys and girls are able to make a better progress in
certain lines of vocational work than their academic
classmates. Their home experience has been different
and their natural aptitude and interest greater. Under
our new plan they are divided into three groups: Beginners, those who are in any work division for the
first time even if they happen to be in the highest grade
in school; dependables, those who are promoted from
the first group because they have shown ability to perform independently the work assigments of the division; and leaders, who can take responsibility in the
division and who can even supervise other pupils while
they work themselves. While our men's meeting is
going on, young leaders are in fact in charge on the
farm and in the different shops.

I am sure I did not really learn very much in any
particular subject until I had begun to teach it; I felt

like a sneak when I accepted my first salary check! And so I feel that this new system of ours has its greatest value in bringing the boys and girls to the point where they can hand on to others something that they have learned. Of course they do not all reach the leadership group. People don't in real life either, but we expect the pupil, before receiving the school certificate, to attain the third group in at least two departments and the second group in all departments to which he has been assigned for two terms.

The plan is doing a lot to place industrial education in the minds of the students. You can see how a new dignity comes to those who enter the dependable or leadership groups. You can see how a new enthusiasm creeps into the work and how impossible it is to keep a boy or girl indefinitely in a department because they can do the work well. That may be a good reason for changing their assignment.

It must be borne in mind that there are definite courses to be covered in each department. The practical work for the girls falls into six divisions, that of the boys into eleven. No pupil can escape trying out all the various activities of the school while he is in training, but on the other hand he is allowed to continue for longer periods in those divisions which he particularly desires. During his school life, Isaiah of today must pass through the poultry division, but if Isaiah is determined to be a carpenter when he leaves school, he can readily be assigned to more terms in that shop. If he looks forward to running his own farm he stays longer in the live-stock and other agricultural divisions. With this flexibility, there is room in the system for sensible training, and also for a training of all the senses as the boy or girl has experience in all the divisions into which the practical work of Penn is divided.

Only less important than the assignment days in our school calendar have become the Fridays after these meetings when the assignments and the standing of each pupil are read before the whole school. No one wants to miss school that morning! The urge is always present to win a place in the group above! or to keep the place already won! There was a surprised Isaiah one morning to find that he was back in the beginners group when he had been promoted to leadership. Leadership means that a sense of responsibility has been developed. Isaiah had walked off from his work in the hot summer term without asking permission or giving explanation to his teacher. From the beginners he had to climb back to his coveted position! And the teacher would be all the more careful to make sure that he actually earned the promotion and that the improvement was not merely skin deep! The system keeps the instructors on the "qui vive" as well as the students.

Another advantage in this plan is that boys and girls of different ages and grades work together. The boy in the beginners group in the dairy is working side by side with a dependable or a leader. He is not allowed to measure the rations or milk the cows, but while he is cleaning the barn, he sees Isaiah do the more advanced work. Perhaps a year later he is again assigned to the dairy, this time a dependable and he comes to it with the background of his experience plus the experience of having watched for ten weeks the work of a leader. When he takes hold to do the more advanced work himself, he knows how it should be done because he unconsciously has absorbed standards of workmanship from the more advanced boy. This is the principle of education in a family where children learn from each other. Here the school becomes a big family!

We anticipate still another advantage although it has not matured in our own experience yet. One reason certain boys and girls go "off island" after they have had the Penn School training is because they need the cash to make a living possible. Our island parents are many of them not in a position to give their children a start in life. Our high-school pupils sometimes drop out because they cannot secure the clothes, books, and other essentials on their road to learning. Younger brothers and sisters require more as the years go on, and when a boy is in his upper 'teens the parents expect him to be earning instead of learning! It is a step in advance taken by a whole community when the big boys and girls stay in school to the finish.

We should like to make it possible for any student in the leadership group to work a year after graduation as an assistant in the shop or on the farm, in the sewing room or home economics department, receiving a regular salary which would make self-support immediate and help them strike roots in our rural community. As only the best records would qualify such young people, it would surely prove an incentive to others. Practical difficulties assert themselves for the salary budget in such a school as this is already necessarily large, and until a money crop is assured to people who can barely make a living under boll weevil conditions there is no great hope that the island itself will be able to support such a plan.

But what of the boys and girls who must earn all or a part of their expenses as they try to finish their course in school? We have that as a daily problem to meet. And we are meeting it in two ways at present. There is work to be done before and after school and on Saturdays which can be kept out of the regular schedule. Pupils who apply for such work are assigned these tasks as paid workers by the hour. They are expected to work as responsible wage earners, and not as a group of beginners with a teacher at their elbow! It was a surprised group of boys who were abruptly turned off last summer term when the farm manager found them playing in the field. They saw others take their places. That was better for them than several sermons on responsibility and honesty!

Then there are the boys who can have no home acre because there is no home equipment or cash for the seed and fertilizer. These are given a piece of land on the study farm; they use the school mule and farm equipment, seed and fertilizer are advanced. They, as well as the school office, must keep track of the cost, and then at the end of the season they can have the crop after deducting the expenses incurred in raising it. Three boys were thus "on their own" last year; each one was given three-fifths of an acre, and with corn selling at $1.00 per bushel one of them had to meet a deficit of three cents, another made $8.85, and one who did the best work made $13.60. This was the first year of the plan, and the race is likely to be better run by that boy who failed in the heat of the summer sun when he tries again. The cash made is, of course, for school expenses.

We have not found it practical under present conditions to adopt the same plan for the girls. In a rural community like ours they are not expected to push out for themselves at so early an age as their brothers. Those who must earn their "school feast" (fees) and a part of their clothing are seen outside of school hours at the ordinary tasks of home makers, work like cleaning and dusting that must be done continually in any home or school.

These most recent developments in the industrial work at Penn have been in the direction of working out a structure, paralleling but not frozen into the academic scheme. The subject divisions, the fees, the grading put the industrial work on a new footing as an educational process; the group system relates it to changing work and aptitudes.

I believe such a plan as ours in which realities take their place beside books, is making for sturdier and more pliant growth. Industrial education can, at the hands of some teachers, become so materialistic that an unfair advantage is taken of the pupil. But the intellectual and spiritual values are there in every task performed, if eyes can see them. And these same values can become a part of the pupil, woven into the very warp and woof of his character because he works with real things—with the forces of nature herself.

Book learning is easy feeding for the mind compared with education correlated with the realities that go to make up living! It takes a greater teacher to teach living than to give merely a so-called "learning." Learning how to live, it seems to me, means liberty and only as we really learn this lesson, can we come out into the glorious freedom of the children of God.

PART III

ACRES FOR CLASSROOMS

I

HE children and the parents call them "School Acres." The teachers call them "Home Acres." There's the thing in a nutshell—the kernel of the third revolution that in the last dozen years has spread from the classrooms of Penn School out onto the farms of St. Helena Island. They are in truth the "Children's Acres," set aside by the parents on their home farms, as part of school work that fits into the rhythm of the island year in bringing the advances in the rural arts to a growing people.

The little homes lie scattered over the plantations, whitewashed and sometimes with charming blue, pink, or lavender trimmings, for the Negro people love color and many of them have not copied the dull customs of the city in their house painting. These homes are all on land which these people own, and here for three generations have the boys and girls trudged from their farms to the school.

For a decade we had been dovetailing the life of our Carolina sea island into our teaching at Penn School, yet there seemed to be many parts of the picture puzzle which would not fit. I have told how we had introduced agriculture among the usual school subjects—but it proved an uneasy bedfellow for arithmetic. We had developed our school farm—but only a small group of boys could work on it. We had started also a miniature farm and demonstration acres so that the children could see the rotation of crops on a small enough scale to make a vivid impression. But plowing and planting and harvest went their courses regardless of the convenience of ours. A growing onion cannot be laid by like a piece of chalk.

More and more we came to realize that for miles

about us were, not miniature farms, but real farms, the sort of farms these children would grow up to, which they were growing up on. And on them swept the sort of years the children would have to master on leaving school. The crop often called the children to the fields at the same time our old Liberty Bell called them to the classroom; and we had that paradox—an agricultural school seemingly in conflict with the farming community it served. The everlasting excuses in the springtime registered this conflict. Parents kept their children out to work in the fields and sometimes only half those enrolled would be in attendance when planting was at its height.

It was in 1917 that we started out definitely hand-in-hand with the seasons, following them—or I might better say, leading them a bit—so that the school year and the island year might coincide. We had occasionally met the crop problem by allowing the children to stay home every other day till the cotton was picked. One year we had given them a special "work week" at home in the spring planting time. The parents had thanked us as if we had given them a personal gift. Now we asked them to coöperate in a plan that would divide the school year into autumn, winter, spring, and summer terms just as their home work was divided. And they responded gladly.

II

AUTUMN

Autumn on the island, as the children see it when they enter school, is a golden time; there are long stretches of yellow marshes and golden brown grass in many fields. The brilliant-colored gum trees, the purple asters growing along the roadsides, the flash of the Kentucky cardinals and their charming whistle, the jolly song of the mocking birds and brown thrashers, all these sights and sounds play upon the consciousness of the boys and girls that cover the roads which lead in from the home farms.

Fields left bare of crops tell of summer's work done. The autumn term begins with October. There are three weeks of the usual school studies before the first call of the fields comes to these country children, the call of the sweet potatoes. We turn the children out, the teachers follow them and while the children work beside their parents and harvest the crop which will help them stay on the road of education during the winter months, the teachers meet them there on their own acres during that home week. All across the island the work goes forward by families. The father or big brother plows up the furrows with the family ox, or pony, or mule. The mother and the children follow with the hoes, and the potatoes are dug and placed in piles to be gathered for the storage. Great banks are made of them—layers of earth piled upon layers of potatoes, till sweet-potato pyramids take their place beside the house or barn ready for the winter's demand.

The visits are expected, as regular schedules are followed by each teacher. With few exceptions the whole family are ready to greet her and the household background becomes a part of her equipment. Experiences in school and at home are talked over; not only is the potato crop of interest, but the past and the coming corn crops, the home garden, the children's record in school. A new understanding takes root. When the teacher has spent an hour in driving to a home, she has a clue as to why Emanuel is sometimes languid in school when he has walked the long miles in the hot sun. When she finds adverse home conditions, she can see why Elizabeth does things that are irritating at school. She gets into the shoes of her children at sweet-potato harvest.

Her immediate purpose, however, is to get the father and mother to set aside a portion of the farm, usually an acre, which the child can handle according to the agriculture lessons he will have in school. Sometimes the parents have not grasped the idea, and the teacher finds the acre a poor one. Joseph had to plant his corn last year in the old potato field, but this year his father gives him the best piece of land on the farm, saying, "We'll get the corn anyway!" when Joseph starts out to win the prize. Pearl has not told about the plan at home; she is a new girl and one who has not caught the new spirit—so the teacher finds no acre selected; the parents still to be convinced. A good acre is given; "right by the road so every one can see it," says the coöperating parent. Argument gives place to enthusiasm when fathers and mothers see that their children mean real work and real crops are grown on those chosen acres.

The acre is measured by the child and the school lessons go home to that particular bit of ground, which often becomes the most interesting plot on the home farm to the parents as well as the children. Results on the farm, in the children, and in the school seem to prove the value of the experiment. In our first years on the island, the only crop that was considered worthy of being measured was cotton; and when, under the school lead, corn was measured and valued and prizes won, it meant new horizons for the island culture. The results, put into figures, influenced the whole community. The children's corn crop was valued at over $3,000 the first year, and over two thousand cans of fruit and vegetables from their acres were recently put up for food in the homes.

These home acres have become our best classrooms. You should go out to Frogmore Plantation where the son of one of the boys in my first class in agriculture at Penn has his acre. This was the father who balked at our early efforts at bringing farming into the school work, but now that same father stands back of his boy and his home acre. It lies directly behind the house, has a neat fence all around it, and is raising crops all the year round now.

Just before the children are turned home for "potato week" they take part in our annual Farmers' Fair, helping to prepare for the exhibits brought in from all the island homes, and showing their own corn, garden stuff, and pigs, and their own handwork done at school. One autumn as I was looking at the coops of chickens that had come in to be judged, I found a small disheveled bird lying at one side with its legs tied together with a calico rag. A small boy stood on the outskirts of the crowd. He had run home, caught his chicken and slipped it in with the others. A sad bunch of feathers it was, but its small owner learned that day something about the better breeding of chickens and how to enter one for an exhibit. The club boys and girls wear a red arm band, front seats are reserved for them, and these farmers-to-be feel their importance on this community feast day. A feast day I call it for always there come to us speakers, from the Department of Agriculture in Washington, our own agricultural college in South Carolina, or other agricultural schools.

The Farmers' Fair has grown so we have instituted
a Junior Farmers' Fair the day before for the younger
boys and girls, only the high school pupils being invited to the grown-ups' fair! And the children's exhibit makes its own picture in its own place. The average yield on our home acres was raised to thirty-one
bushels of corn when the average in the state was
seventeen bushels. The prize winner one year had ma-
terial for her English work when she wrote the following composition:

> I am going to tell you about my prize acre. The first thing
> I did was to select my corn seed while it was being harvested.
> I put some lime on it so the weevils could not destroy it, when
> I hung it up in the barn. In December my ground was plowed.
> There are five reasons why our prize acre should be plowed
> in the fall. First, so that the insects can be exposed and die;
> second, so that the rubbish can be turned under and decay;
> third, it saves time; fourth, the animals are stronger; fifth, it
> helps to hold moisture
> In March I tested my corn seed. The subject of one of our
> lessons was, "Test, don't guess!" If we test our corn seed it
> will save time, save land, and save seed. I planted my corn
> in drill, then thinned it to one stalk in every hill. I cultivated
> my corn every five days until it got about three feet high.
> Then I cultivated it once every ten days. I lay my corn by
> with a sweep. I won the first prize last year because I had the
> highest yield. My corn yield was sixty-six bushels and six
> quarts on this acre. I hope it will double this year, and I know
> it will double if I try.

But some of the children do not have a fair chance
to win a prize at the Farmers' Fair. Their parents may
be slow to grasp the plan the first year, and give them
a poor acre. To offset this discouragement a Beat-
Your-Record prize is given. And the boy who raised
only twelve bushels on his acre last year wins the

prize this year with fifty-one bushels for the family corn house.

After "potato week" the children come back into the scheme of everyday schooling. But the school life has been influenced by that home week; the home acre is the basis of the agricultural lessons. In every classroom you will find a large chart bearing the name of each child, and on that chart the date his compost pile is started at home, the date the acre is plowed. So compost pile and plow take their proper place with blackboard and lead pencil.

III

WINTER

Our marshes turn brown, but the woodlands the children pass as they trudge to school during the winter term are as green as ever with the Cuban pines, the loblollies, and the great long-needle pines. These and the evergreen leaves of the live oaks and the water oaks with their swinging gray moss, would make you forget the season were it not for the cold winds that can sweep across the island. The gum trees are bare, and the red oaks, but their branches are garnished with great bunches of green mistletoe. There is the occasional holly and the very common cassina with bright red berries to add their jolly bit of winter color. The children call the cassina the "Christmas berry." They see the herons, the snipe, and the divers of the marsh lands and tidal rivers; they hear the marsh hen and the whir of quail disturbed by their feet in the brush. They pass the old cotton fields with their dead brown stalks, for the most part rough and unkempt, and broken only where the hogs have been nosing for small nuts at the roots of the wire grass.

For the islands have never had the custom of fall and winter plowing. In plantation days, when the cotton was picked, the land was always allowed to stand till the springtime. Then great bonfires would tell of the return of the men to the fields ready to plow for the new cotton crop. This old system of one-crop farming did not mean an all-year job for the men and boys. The cotton habit had its grip on two generations after freedom. It has been no easy matter for the Penn School boys and girls to get their parents to see the need for plowing their home acres before spring, just as it has been no easy matter for teachers and farm demonstrators to get our farmers to adopt it generally. But the one has helped the other, and of a winter's day plowed spots can be seen all over the island where the new idea has broken through.

The gala time in the autumn when the old and young come together at the Farmers' Fair is matched in the wintertime by our Christmas celebrations. I remember one old Negro who said, "Oh, yes, we has Christmas Eve, Christmas Eve's Eve and Christmas, Christmas Adam, and Christmas Madam!" He was remembering the Christmas week of freedom from work and general jollification on the plantation in slavery days. We hold to about as many days of celebration in our community school. And meanwhile, throughout December, in anticipation of them, every child from the six-year-olds to the young people in their twenties, is making a gift that will go home for the holidays, and every school department is in league with the festival.

Christmas in the country, and particularly on our sea island, is the time for boys and girls who have left the

islands to return; it is always the best of times in the
church, at the school, and in the homes; the air is full
of the Christmas spirituals and the Christmas carols.
I remember the first Christmas I had on the island. We
had arranged to have Santa Claus suddenly appear on
the platform to the ringing of sleigh bells. I shall never
forget the sensation as we heard—I had almost said,
felt—the children draw in their breaths all at once.
There were about two hundred and fifty of them and
one might have been in a forest on a windy day. One of
the boys wrote home to another island where there had
never been a Christmas celebration of the sort:

> I would like to know how you all enjoyed your Christmas.
> Why, I had a good time because I saw something I had never
> seen before. I saw Santa Claus walking across the floor, and
> I had never seen him before. What you think about that? It
> pays a man, my mother, to leave home sometimes and he will
> see more and learn more.

A Christmas mystery play is given in our large hall
where the great rafters and rough finish exactly fit the
play; and where some fifty players, teachers and boys
and girls, give this old form of the Christmas story.
But of that I shall write in a later chapter.

Christmas over, as the winter months pass, the charts
in the classrooms begin to tell their story. Perhaps
there are homes that are not in step with the plan.
Either the child is lazy or indifferent, or the parent is
holding back, not realizing that the agricultural work
at school is to help the whole family at home. The
empty spaces on the chart are silent teachers. Other
children's fall and winter plowing has been done, the
compost piles started, and the agriculture class is
headed by boys and girls whose school agriculture has

gone home and whose home acres have reached the higher standard.

IV

SPRING

At last the first buds burst. The sand flies tell us spring is here; the drum fish are biting; the marshes take on a green color; the spring tide covers the road in places so that boys and girls must occasionally wade through, and may even have to take to the boats. The smell of brown earth is everywhere as the plows get busy; the live oaks drop their winter leaves as new ones push them off. The ground beneath looks like autumn, but the trees themselves fairly shout for spring as they don their new lettuce-colored green. The road to Land's End is bordered with pink and white phlox for miles, and in the woods you see the wild azaleas and dog wood. The yellow jessamine mounts high in the tall pines. The boys wear it to school in their buttonholes, and the girls fasten it in their hair. A little later Cherokee roses clamber over vines and roadside thickets, peach trees are in bloom, and wild plum bushes sweeten the air on every side. There is a call to the land in the smell of the brown earth.

And Penn School children respond. The new spring schedule begins with a school frolic. Farming must be inoculated with fun. We started off that first spring of 1918 with a parade and have kept it up since. Down the oyster-shell road to the crossroads store they marched with only trees and marshes for onlookers, but they walked as proud and straight as if they were on Fifth Avenue. The boys in their blue overalls carried hoes

Philip, a high school boy who wants to be a farm demonstration agent.

and rakes over their shoulders; many of the girls also. Those in the Canning Club brandished empty cans. Occasionally a banner was held aloft with such legends as "Plant and Protect," or "Corn Will Win." Many of the boys could not achieve blue overalls as they had to wear out their old suits, so it was a motley parade, all sizes, all colors, but all enthusiasm. Here was Freezie, whose "basket-name" tells us he was born in the time of an unusual cold snap. That year he won the pure-bred cockerel sent down from Hampton for our Farmers' Fair. There was Collins Washington, whose home acre was fenced and who was out to win the prize pig. Here were Netha and Rose Cuthbert, and Isabella Coleman, girls who walked twelve and fourteen miles a day till there was room in the dormitory for them. There was Ezekiel, in a gorgeous blue sweater from that last "barrel of gold" sent down by city friends to our little sales house. "Affliction is mo' dan a match fo' a pusson," one mother had said when she came to see if some sweet potatoes would secure needed shoes and jacket. The cotton raised that season, she explained, would pay only their taxes and the corn would hardly feed the family. But her boys marched that day in the parade; and perhaps democracy has as good a chance on St. Helena as anywhere else in America.

Down the road came the children led by the band and the colors; some of the band boys in uniform and some not, for we have never had enough uniforms to go around. The joy in the whole performance was measured by the fact that the "faraways" who had been given permission to leave the parade at the store so as to cut short their long walk home, countermarched with the others and refused to drop out till they were back in the school grove.

Always Planting Week means a picnic; and that means a bit of lunch, baseball on the athletic field, folk games in the grove, relay races on the playground, and laughter everywhere. But the picnic and parade are more than just a frolic. They are gotten up each year by the boys and girls of the agriculture clubs as a send-off to Planting Week and the spring term. The day after sees all the older boys and girls helping their fathers and mothers on the home farms. Now it is, also, that they sow their own acres, and start in competition to win first place for actual production.

When we started the home-acre week, all the children were in the Corn Club, but as time has gone on, we have developed a Peanut Club, a Garden Club which is made up of the older girls, and the Progressive Young Farmers' Club—an older group of boys, who have advanced to poultry and pigs. Here again we have emphasized food crops to loosen the grip of the one-crop system of farming. Under that system the whole family devoted all its time and energy to the growing of long-staple cotton—an economy which meant neither all-the-year-round work for the men, nor all-the-year food for their families. As a result, food needed for the household and feed for live stock was bought at the stores of the cotton merchant. Fortunately for St. Helena, the heads of the firms of island merchants in the decades following the war between the states, have been just and generous friends to the Negro and tried to protect the farmers when they were too ignorant to protect themselves from the evils of the credit system. None the less, here as elsewhere in the cotton lands, the merchants fed the people during the winter with food-stuffs—that they themselves should have grown on their farms—in exchange for some of the cotton they turned in to these same stores. This system at its best means poverty, poor food, poor homes, poor morals, and poor health. So in Planting Week as in the agricultural clubs, in the Farmers' Fair and demonstration acres, our All-Year Country School has been trying to open the way for crop rotation and the variety of crops that would bring scientific farming and business methods to every farm.

In contrast with many a country school where only a handful of children turn up, our boys and girls are back at their desks when Planting Week is over. Their parents have come to coöperate so heartily that our average attendance throughout the remainder of the spring is as good as at any season. Planting Week is followed by "home days" which make it possible for the family to keep up with the crops in the field. When we began the new schedule we closed the classrooms every other day. That proved to be unnecessary, and we have found that two home days in the week are enough. Our youngest day pupils are not included in the schedule lest it might easily revert to child labor were they also sent out on the home days. But nature study for the very little ones, and a school acre for the pupils in the fourth grade, prepare them for home work when they are old enough.

Exhibition day comes as a climax to the spring term —well named—for on that day every year the entire school comes before the people. Then are life and learning dramatized; then can be seen the joy of work and struggle. The old tradition of the academic exhibitions has been preserved, but transmuted. The people all come, some returning from long distances inland and some from other islands. The merchants close their stores; it is the school's day! All the white people come,

and from noon till sunset the crowd owns the school.
One year we put 260 children on the stage in a Carnival
of Industries! And it was a carnival! "Uncle Sam"
brought the different industries before the audience—
King Corn with his farmers who were the Corn Club
boys; King Cotton with a crowd of cotton pickers;
King Wheat from the west with his cowboys who came
dashing in with their whips cracking. I can't begin to
tell you all about it.

Agriculture came on as a play—"The Soil Builders
and the Soil Robbers." The children personified the different crops. They told the farmer how they had been
exhausting his soil all these years. They called for the
demonstration agent, who showed the farmer how he
could rotate them. Corn, cotton, and sweet potato children marched in a swinging drill. Even the tree crop
was not forgotten and the young pine trees added their
bit of color and beauty and their own lesson to the
scene. The play ended with all the children singing
"Whistle and Hoe," as they cultivated their acres.

At another exhibition, the graduating class were
shown at their school work on the platform. They sang
and they worked and then each one spoke for about
two minutes as a demonstration was given. Corn seed
was tested, a cow was milked, a horse shod. The carpenters were building; the blacksmiths were welding
a tire. Of the girls one was cutting and fitting a dress;
another was at the sewing machine; a third was cooking; a fourth was making a rag rug at the loom; and in
a corner a fifth was teaching a class of children.

Penn School boys spend about half of the time on
the farm and in the shops that are necessary to farm
life; Penn School girls, about half of their time in household duties including sewing. The Penn School Certifi-

cate stands for the work that has been done by each pupil. Every certificate is likely to be different, for besides "farming" and "housekeeping" are written in the special work done by each graduate. The certificates are given at exhibition time. Each bears the picture of the road of live oaks which has been traveled by three generations of Penn School children and which, as one of the children said, shows the light at the end of it. There are the usual words about "certifying" and "satisfactorily completing"; but the really significant words follow: "and has shown a spirit of trustworthiness, service to the islands, and loyalty to the ideals of Penn School."

This spirit was tested when the call went to Caesar who was trying to earn money for a short course at Hampton and to get some modern equipment for his own farm. He was earning forty dollars a week and he came back to the island to take a county school that sorely needed a teacher. The salary offered was thirty-five dollars a month! "I will start on Tuesday" was his reply to the message telling him of the need of his people.

Group spirit, character building, and individual initiative go forward along with practical results which in themselves seem to warrant our experiment.

V

SUMMER

Summer comes and the marshes are as green as the cornfields. It gets hot enough to "cook an aig in de sand"! The nonpareils find their way to the island, flitting about like flashes of the rainbow, with their red breasts, their rich blue heads, the yellow and green on their bodies and wings. When they appear, all work stops as we watch them dart about in search of food. They are one of the compensations for the hot days! Insects seem to fill the air. Cockroaches as large as small mice have to be fought in the house; creeping things of every description try to take possession; and one evening we had to give up our living-room, as flying ants had taken it for their own.

Our summer session, the first year, had to be built up from the bottom, for, under our new four-season program, classroom subjects and other industrial work had given way to agriculture during the first spring term.

Remembering the long walks on the sandy roads, we decided to try a schedule that would bring the children in before the heat of the day. School was called at six-thirty in the morning. It was well named "sunrise school"! One of the boys fell asleep in his class the week before the summer term began. We found that he had been practicing waking up early every morning so as to be on time when "sunrise school" began! Another who walked in from a home farm located so far away that he had to start before "dayclean," wrote, "I gets up just when a farmer should get up. It is just a pleasure walk for me before the sun rises." And a third said, "I like this school. It comes at the waking up of the brains."

There were disadvantages in the early school, however. Parents began to ask us to change the time. In summer, the old plantation roads are overgrown with weeds and grasses, sometimes reaching almost as high as the head. Starting before the dew was off these roads, the children would be wet through before reaching the school. So we returned to the old hour of opening which seemed to fit the greater number. And spending half of the time of the summer session in the shop or kitchen or sewing-room, and half of the time in the classrooms, brought the children farther along in their studies than they had been able to go by the old schedule with its long vacation.

Like the big community gatherings which mark each of the earlier school terms—Farmers' Fair in the autumn, the Christmas festival in the winter, planting-week picnic, and exhibition in the spring—so a dramatic climax is reached at the end of the summer term when the school has its watermelon picnic. Then is the time to see our country school. The big wagon comes in from the fields loaded with the luscious melons. The children have "thrown up" five cents apiece and can eat all the melon they want. Barrels are provided at convenient places for the rinds. No utensils are needed. Shining dark eyes, and shining white teeth cutting through the delicious pink of the melons, are a sight to remember. Now one learns the real way to eat a melon! One learns how a real melon tastes. None of these ice-cold slices served up on a plate from a melon that has traveled miles, can give the slightest idea of the real thing! A melon kissed by the hot sun and eaten as nature intended, fresh from the field, is one of the greatest joys of a country school in the South. It is a compensation that a sea islander is well satisfied with.

And when the boys and girls go home for the brief vacation so that all the teachers may have a rest, there is an immediate desire for the school to reopen. For it has come about that this school is one where the pupils do not long for vacations.

When Charles Dickens drew the picture of Dotheboys Hall in "Nicholas Nickleby," he foretold the coming of industrial education. "How do you spell winder?" called out the master, and when the answer came w-i-n-d-e-r, the trembling boy was ordered to "go wash that winder!" Our children make their own connections, for fun and farming have at least a bowing acquaintance.

VI

In such a scheme as ours, the whole school is brought into team play. The out-of-classroom work of the teachers requires equipment. The blacksmithing and wheel-wrighting shops have built the gig, the buckboard, and the buggy; the harness-making shop has made most of the harness. Ford cars now take their part in the plan and the boys and men in the Cope shops keep them in order.

While all the teachers go out on a regular schedule, there are four members of the staff whose work keeps them fairly constantly in the field. The demonstration agent meets the farmers in their fields and barnyards. The cooking teacher joins the nurse in home visits, for there is often a close connection between home diet and the "underweights," and between underweight and petty illness that may keep Benola or Manche home from school. Home Improvement Clubs have been organized on many of the plantations. Our normal teacher goes out to the crossroad county schools two days in the week to help teachers struggling with sixty and eighty children and no equipment.

To find the right teachers is our most difficult problem in all of this work. By that I mean that there are few rurally-minded teachers. Compensations must be found in the work itself in such an isolated community. And the work calls for far more than the usual school. When the home and the farm become a part of the school equipment, the teachers encounter the questions of men, women, and children who have been farmers all their lives. We try to meet these difficulties by teachers' meetings organized under the demonstration agent, himself an expert and one who has done the job first as a boy on his father's farm on Ladies Island, then in Penn School, then at Hampton, and now as a worker with the workers, always studying to keep a little ahead of the game. Every visit is reported on at these meetings, questions are taken up, and right answers are carried back to those homes. It is a different thing to study about agriculture even in such schools as Hampton and Tuskegee and to know the practical vicissitudes of corn and cotton and food crops on farm after farm. A teachers' acre of corn gives Penn teachers the hang of the tools and words necessary for their out-of-door classrooms.

Our teachers start out for the plantations at the close of one of these meetings where the experiences of the last visits have been reviewed and where a report of each child has been given to show the progress and the spirit of that child, his farm, and his home. It is the early morning and they have their lunch boxes. The "chariot" carries them to certain points from which they set out on their calls. The individual and the community must advance together and the appeal to boys and girls is lost if living conditions are impossible. We are more nearly beginning at the right end of things when each teacher becomes a student of how to reclaim those conditions. If missionary effort means to redeem the lives of men, an agricultural school in a rural community is concrete Christianity.

In spite of the old drag of poverty, of an outworn single-crop system, of the coming of the boll weevil, we have had a special vantage ground in our work on St. Helena where the people own their own farms, compared with communities where the parents are wage earners on the new big truck farms of the South and the farmers want cheap child labor. Freedom is easily lost. A young teacher wrote to me in great distress. She had been warned that if she attempted to lengthen her short four months' school term the truck farmer who wanted children in his lettuce fields would see to it that she lost her school the following season. So far as education goes the situation could be improved if all country schools could adapt their schedules to the growing crops.

When we compare Penn School with the typical county school of the cotton lands we get a true measure of what such a rounded scheme of education means. In the average county school on the sea islands, in a room that is rough and cheerless, a large group of ungraded children gather, sometimes eighty pupils for one teacher to handle. Painted boards serve as blackboards, rough benches hold the crowd, and when a class is called, it is something of a marvel to see the boys and girls climb out without making their neighbors move from their seats. The greatest failure of the county school has been that it does not give the pupils ambition to go farther. They drop out after they have sat through three or four terms and often they prove the old adage that a little knowledge is a dangerous thing. A four to six months' term hardly gives time for the subjects to go round and yet it seems remarkable to see how many children learn in spite of these poor conditions.

Down the road comes a boy, barelegged, riding on a horse; no bridle, only a rope to guide the animal, a big ax on his shoulder, and he comes down the road at a swift gallop. He represents the native strength of the sea-island Negro. But his strength is all in his body. A four months' term in the county school for three or four years will scarcely enable him to qualify as literate.

Here down the same road come the boys and girls from their club work on our home acres. Their parents are standing back of them; the whole family has part in the all-year school, and strength of intellect is being added to those strong bodies. The home, the farm, and the shop have all yielded their experiences to enrich the life of the child. A great task is thrown upon the school to coördinate all of these agencies and to keep a proper balance. We are sure of making blunders, but we feel the enthusiasm of being on the right road. Joe Wyne spoke truly when he said of the Corn Club: "That plan is very patienceable. It will sure stir up the young blood on farming."

The children's pride in their school has been growing and is very real.

I must not forget to tell you about my corn and how it is getting along [wrote Aurelius when I was off island during the heat of summer]. When you left, it was about five feet tall; now it's from seven and one-half to nine feet tall and it is still growing. I sowed peas in my corn alley on the twenty-fourth of June and it is about two or three inches high. Wish you could see it now.

Another letter brought me the message:

We have been having some warm days since you have been gone, but we are getting along all right. The sand is just like fire has been on it. And when I go barefooted it burns my feet and then I run in the shade to cool them. On Wednesday, I put soda around the corn's roots and after that I thinned the corn so there wouldn't be too much in one hill. I hope I will be successful in this corn contest. I should like that prize.

And James described his field: "You can stay a far distance off and the large green field is all in bloom. It is a pretty sight and the people look at my corn."

The month of June was very hot, but we came through victoriously. [wrote Benjamin and he continued] I wish you could see my crop and we are all working to make good in the class room too, and the Cubs (the baseball nine of the summer) have not lost a game yet since you went away.

Unknowingly he showed the balance of work, study, and play that we are striving for in planning the day's work for the island boys and girls.

"The mountains these people of the mud flats have to climb are spiritual," wrote a guest to the island. And I believe there is a spiritual development when education increases the ability to do creative work, whether in the classroom, in the shop, or on the farm.

But our mountains are far from being conquered. Every year reveals new undergrowth to be cleared; old issues must be met on new levels. The sweeping significance of the change only unfolded as, step by step, we made the home acres our classrooms. Serious administrative problems had to be met in advance. At the start we went to Dr. Hollis B. Frissell of Hampton Institute, and almost before we had outlined the plan he urged us to put it into operation. He saw the vision of a rural school that fitted into the needs of a rural community. From him we went to Dr. Wallace Buttrick, then president of the General Education Board, with a request for a grant to help meet the cost of the longer terms and summer supervision, of salaries, equipment, and wear and tear. In his high office, overlooking the harbor of New York, we talked it over with that educator of delightful humor and earnestness, full of the desire to help the whole world but able to see the needs of a small island community off the coast of South Carolina. As a result, the board was convinced that here was an experiment in rural education worth trying, and it made annual grants ranging from $5,000 to $10,000 to get it well started. The further continuance of the demonstration now hangs on our ability to get adequate support for it from new sources.

Ours is still a living experiment which must go forward in its island laboratory if it is to prove a practicable and possible way out for some of the problems confronting rural education everywhere. We have been breaking new ground since 1917, but time is needed for cultivation. We feel as if only the rough plowing had been done during these dozen years. We had no patterns to copy, for we knew of no other rural community where such an educational experiment was being made. On St. Helena we are attempting to demonstrate what life can mean for old and young where people hold or have recovered their lives and livelihood.

When the home could be relied upon to yield a knowledge of life's realities, the school could depend upon books as its only tools. That day is past for the white child. It never existed for the Negro child. "I know I would like to read" sang the parents of an older day, and the refrain repeats itself in the spiritual as in their hearts and minds. We have seen that school meant one thing to them, the reading of books, but they are slowly realizing that education must mean a combination of life's experiences. And those boys and girls whose parents stand back of the school are the ones to hand on what comes to them.

> Yours is de best-hewn plan fo' we people [said a parent at one of our meetings]. Dis Parents' League is necessary to change brains wid each other. I am sure proud ob my chillun in school. An' dey gib me glad fo' dey eddycashun. I tells yo', I hab to stan' on my toe wid dem.

An all-year school, all-community school, a rural school that moves with the four seasons on the farms and that touches the whole life of the people, must look forward to a series of years—I cannot tell how many—to prove itself. So that plans made may be the "best-hewn for the people."

PART IV

THE GROWN FOLKS COME TO SCHOOL

PENN SCHOOL has been an adventure in adult education from the beginning. On June 18, 1862, the first class came to school, nine men and women who had been only field hands and to whom all "learnin'" was as magic. Their number grew rapidly, the children naturally came with their parents, so in August we find the school organized with "the oldest class, the middle class, the youngest, and the adult class." Necessity was certainly the Mother of Invention in that school organization of the sixties. And the philosophy back of the invention holds for Penn School today where we are reaching the farmers and their wives, indirectly through the children and their home acres, and directly through community class, midwives' class, home-makers' clubs, through Farmers' Fair and demonstration work, coöperative society and credit union, all now brought to focus through our Community House.

When twenty-five years ago we built the new schoolhouse, which climbed up into the air two stories and gave to many their first journey upstairs, the grownups wanted to come to school too. Mothers and grandmothers made up the first of our adult groups in the modern Penn School. They called themselves the Community Class and after a checkered career in sewing, knitting, basketry, and Bible lessons, they settled down to an ever new and interesting course in hygiene and home nursing given by the school nurse, and with talks on everything under the sun given irregularly by the principal.

This weekly connection with the school has made them a link with the whole island for we have no local newspapers and the women carry out the news, at least in headlines, to their plantations. They do not come just to get for themselves, either, for as they sing the island spirituals after their "lessons," they sew busily on the quilt which will find its way to some home where there is great need: "Some one wussuh off dan we!"— and many a time do they "throw up the collection" for the sick member or for some community call. Once a month you will find a merry crowd "Going to Jerusalem" or trying to pin the tail on the donkey amid shouts of laughter. Games learned in the Community Class go out and add spice to the home in the country.

The class meets in the library, as do all our smaller groups of adults, and so they sit surrounded by books which will be open to their children but are closed to many of the older generation. Books exert a silent influence on these older folk whose hard life on the farm has left little time to keep on with the things they learned in the old schoolhouse. So long as schoolgirls or schoolboys are learning far in advance of their parents so that there is a gulf instead of a bridge between them, a lot of our education can fall by the wayside. But when they find those parents keeping abreast of the times, too, the whole family are "climbing upstairs" together.

The demonstration method is the most effective working principle in this phase of rural education as in all others. The education that goes home is what really counts. "You have opened my eyes, and I wish I could go back twenty years," said one of the club women when she showed us her hundred pure-bred Rhode Island Red chickens raised from the clutch of eggs and the four hens and one rooster she had purchased at the school. When our cooking teacher became the home demonstration agent, home-makers' clubs organized themselves on the different plantations. The boll weevil

brought household problems no less than crop problems in its train. The shift to food crops would not have
gotten very far if our island cooks and canners had not
been enlisted in the revolution. It brought home to the
school as never before that there must be an educated
motherhood as well as an educated fatherhood if children are to have their chance.

I said the home-makers' clubs organized themselves.
Yes, that is the way it is done. The teacher talks with
one of the women on the plantation who has shown an
interest in the work. She sees her neighbors and they
come together for a meeting called in one of the homes.
"I listen to as many of the women as would like to
talk, after we have opened with devotions, and then I
tell them about club work and we elect our officers," is
the brief description of the organizing given by the
teacher. This seems very simple, and right in those
words, "I listen," lies its philosophy. Teaching too
often is talking before the ground is plowed and cultivated and so the harvest is necessarily meager. Instead
of trying to fit a cut-and-dried plan to each club, the
members talk over what they want and the plan fits
those desires.

Gardens have come to the front—especially since the
coming of the "bo' evil!" So the club works on how to
make the corn, okra, bean, and tomato plots better.
Gardens on St. Helena had their beginnings in the cotton rows, for there was to be found the only fertilized
land; tomatoes began their struggling existence in competition with the cotton. Tomatoes lead the van among
the kitchen crops, for they are easily grown and easily
preserved for winter use.

You will hear these clubs talking about the kind of
meals they are serving and "a balanced menu" has come

into their vocabularies. Chickens and eggs for home
and shipping are brought up; how to improve the
kitchen, and of course there are the lessons in canning,
preserving, and pickling. But there are also discussions
on the church and Sunday school attendance, on venti-
lation, demonstrations in renewing shabby furniture,
dressmaking, and the care of babies. The school nurse
and the home demonstration agent work in coöperation, and cleaned-up yards, bedroom contests, flower
gardens, all have a place. If you were to run down the
list of subjects taken up in the course of a year by these
club women you would literally go from A to Z, and in
the program you would find listed and celebrated an
"Achievement Day" which helps to give a visual exhibit of their efforts and beats any of the usual, prosy,
written club reports. Not all the women in the clubs
are parents of Penn School children, nor are all the
parents of the children in the clubs, but the yeast is
working on many plantations.

These farm women have always worked in the fields
by the side of their men. As education moved forward,
the home began to come into its own, so the hard mo-
notony on the acres of cotton has become varied with
the gardens, the canning, the sewing, the meetings at
the school and in the homes,—and many an island
woman now not only has her pantry well stocked with
canned vegetables and fruit but keeps as many engage-
ments in the course of a week as her city cousin. You
would find her trudging with her young people the
long miles in the evening to see the Christmas Mystery
Play at the school, find her at the local canning club
meeting (we call them Home-makers Clubs nowadays),
and at the local Parents Association; find her always

deep in her own little community but with her mind facing the school to let no new idea escape!

Outside the home, the vocation open to the island women who have had Penn training is school-teaching. Let me introduce you to one of them. Just on the edge of "the Main" is Florine Washington; she will always be affectionately called "Miss Florine." She is teaching in a two-roomed schoolhouse which was built entirely by the people themselves. I might add that the carpentry work was done by one of the first boys to get that training at Penn. Here has she transplanted the community idea, working through her church and boys and girls clubs, circulating books from the collection sent to her school from our Library, and meeting with the other home makers in her own home or theirs. She is always ready to pass on what has come to her, and eager to get her best pupils into Penn. We are not a boarding school but we do try to fit in her "graduates," when we can, although they are not islanders.

In the days of slavery, the midwives held a most honorable place on the plantations. They were given careful teaching, some of them being sent "to Charleston," I've been told, "to get lessons," and the "trade" was handed down in a family of slaves with great care. It was a vital link in the chain! With freedom came disorganization and with no supervision or special training many a midwife traveled far from the ideals of her mother and grandmother of the old slave street. No records were kept of births and deaths when we first came to St. Helena, but we knew too many babies died and too many began life with a handicap.

Our school nurse had been giving suggestions to such midwives as belonged to our community class, but when South Carolina passed a law that all practi-

tioners should receive instruction and be forced to hold
a state certificate, a class of midwives came into being,
and now with its monthly meetings and high standards
of work, mothers and babies are feeling the benefit of
this group in our scheme of adult education. They are
very proud of their blue uniforms, "jes like Dr. Nuss!"
and of their nursing bags which are regularly inspected
and supplied from our nurse's office. The monthly
meeting is not enough, and a genuine step was taken
when we were able to give intensive training to one of
the midwives for a three months' period. She walks in
from her home to the school every day, just as the children do, and forms a practical class of one in midwifery.

I met Nurse Brisbane the day she entered in training.
"Dis is de greates' day I eber seen on St. Helena," she
said, "de greates' day! And my own parents ain't neber
seen dis day! I walk an' walk dis day, an' yet I ain't tire.
I see my limbs git lighter and lighter fo' I see de
Greater Day a-comin'!" I believe it is coming and when
a survey made recently under Dr. Thomas J. Woofter,
Jr., of the Research Department of the University of
North Carolina, showed our infant mortality to be
forty-eight per one thousand, we realized the tangible
results of this effort to lift the old service to new estate.

II

Our "campaigns" for better homes on St. Helena and
all the islands have made up an adventure in adult education which also can be measured. A letter came from
Washington asking us to join in the national movement
and a new thrill was given to the very common tasks
of women in our island homes.

Nurse Brisbane, a member of the midwives' class.

The outline sent gave us all the suggestions we needed! There were committees for everything! Publicity, home surroundings, home equipment, home furnishings and decorating, home budget, the reception of visitors, and program of events. The young Negro men and women on these committees had heard their own grandparents tell of that not-so-very-far-away time— if we measure time as the Orient does—when individual family life was unknown on the islands.

These young people completely furnished and exhibited a little cottage that stood on the school grounds, borrowing what they could from the homes and stores. The budget was worked out so that everyone might know the cost of the house, the furnishings, and also the general expenses of the imaginary family that lived in the house—a good connection this with the arithmetic in the schoolrooms. For a week a better home was the subject of conversation in hundreds of island homes. A demonstration week followed the work of the committee, and a program each afternoon (begun of course by the school band playing "Home Sweet Home") focused attention on costs, sanitation, the arrangement of flowers and pictures, books in the homes, and play.

When the following letter came down from Washington, the Department of Commerce, Office of the Secretary, St. Helena was probably the happiest community in the whole country! Let me quote the letter:

It gives me real pleasure to inform you that St. Helena has won the third prize, $50.00, for having one of the best demonstration houses in the 1922 Better Homes in America Campaign.

In behalf of the Advisory Council, I wish to convey the feeling that you [Miss House, the assistant principal, had served as Chairman of the Whole] and the men and women who served with you, have merited the gratitude of your community and the appreciation of the whole country for having set the standard for other cities to follow.

The work you and your committee have done to improve the living condition of the Negro citizens in South Carolina is an inspiration and a challenge to all of us.

We were especially interested in the budget worked out for the furnishing of the cottage and for the monthly maintenance. This was one of the features which finally placed your report among the prize-winners.

It may interest you to know that 961 communities observed Better Homes Week this first year of the campaign. We hope St. Helena will be represented annually in this important work, and that you will carry out the very interesting program you have suggested.

Yours faithfully,
Herbert Hoover

We did carry out our program the next year, and a second prize was won! Enthusiasm soared! Even the youngest were full of the idea. Here is a bit written by a third grader:

I am going to have a home, yes, a home. And what kind of a home do you think I am going to have? A better home, yes, a better home and I am going to see that I have my windows washed, walls papered and floors scrubbed and old tin cans buried, and my wood pile in the back yard, horse stable cleaned out and a lawn and plenty of flowers planted and a garden and a gig shelter.

In order to have better homes we must follow rules, we must have everything clean about us. I am going to plant two trees in front of my yard.

We have gone on year after year and always has come the letter from Washington—two from the President himself!—bringing good news; a second prize, then a special first (won on a complete better home suited to the purse and needs of the island; built by the boys and furnished by the girls, and committees helping all along the line), and three honorable mentions. In the last "campaign" there were over 5,900 American communities in the competition. As the work has spread throughout the country, St. Helena has done her best to keep in step; and to win something every year has served to deepen the local interest. But the winning was the lesser of the goods wrought by the campaigns. Their influence has put its stamp on hundreds of island homes.

When we met the people in the church last autumn, Miss House told them about our visit to the White House in June to meet Mrs. Hoover and to tell her about our better homes campaigns. She had sent a message to the islanders: "Tell them I should like to see them some time. I should like to visit St. Helena." When Miss House had finished, Dennis Freeman, one of the old men, arose. "We doesn't often have a message from the President's wife," he said, "and I mek a motion dat we all stan' on our feet and show our thanks." They did so and then the preacher rose to the occasion: "You all know the President's wife is the First Lady of the Land," said he, "and if she comes to see us, she'd be the First Lady of the Island, and the First Lady of the Church too!" When told of this vote of thanks Mrs. Hoover sent her thanks to the people for "conferring upon her these 'titles.'" The letter was read at our community sing and the White House seemed quite close to the island!

These campaigns for better homes for our island community had a counterpart in the rearing of a better home for the community work itself. If you ever tried to fit adult activities into an ordinary schoolhouse you know what it means to shift classes to make room for the grown-ups on certain days in the week, and how difficult it all is! We did this for years, until finally our Community House was built by the side of the road, opposite one of our churches. There were three hundred men and women in line in the various clubs and classes which marched in and took possession when it was dedicated. That was one of the gladdest days on the island.

For over a year a huge pile of oyster shells had stood near the site. The oxcarts had brought the shells at a time when we could have them hauled with the least expense. We called them our Pile of Faith! Finally the money needed was accumulated to put the shells in motion and a start was made. "The Pile of Faith" was mixed with sand brought from Jericho (our own sand is not sharp enough for concrete construction), and cement brought from "the Main." Island muscles did the work under the leadership of two Penn School graduates who had taken the full course in the carpentry shop at Hampton.

I remember going out that first day about noontime. The men had just knocked off and were sitting in the shade of the live oaks. I heard them singing. And they were singing spirituals. I saw the huge hole in the ground their shovels had been making that morning. In the middle Thaddeus had stuck a long pole, and from its end there fluttered a red rag, below that a piece of white cloth, and next to that the blue! Here seemed to be a group of laborers fired with the thought that they were starting no ordinary building, and the improvised flag as well as the spirituals told passers-by something of the meaning that underlay the building of the house.

A busy building it is! At one end are our library rooms, easily made into three sections by the closing of wide doors, so that small groups can meet in rooms that fit their size. In the large central room the school gathers for its noon chapel service, and on Sunday evenings. Here you may hear the community sings every third Sunday; on Saturday evenings you will see the play parties, or perhaps happen in on an evening of prize declamations or debates. And here are held the meetings which make the Community House what its name implies.

At the far end is a dining room, with its small round tables graced with flowers or greens. Every school day are served the hot school lunches cooked by the girls themselves, and around the tables sit the boys and girls learning almost unconsciously those lessons in amenities needed in every home. The kitchen is one of the most beautiful rooms in the house, and home making is learned that can travel from the Community House to the island farms.

Surely there could not be a more beautiful memorial to Hollis Burke Frissell, made possible by the gifts of his friends of both races. I do not remember just what spiritual was sung that first morning but it might well have been:

> I'm a-goin' to build
> Right on dis shore,
> Yes, I'm a-goin' to build
> Right on dis shore
> Right on dis shore
> I'm a-goin' to build fo' muh Mastuh
> Fo' muh Mastuh till I die.

III

When, twenty-four years ago, we set off down the oyster-shell roads on Wonder and Wander, our ponies had not taken us far before we saw that the island farming was a family job; mother, father, and children working together. And, as in time those trips carried us deeper into the island life, the educational bearing of what we saw slowly unfolded itself before us. In the North, throughout Colonial times and after, the New England school had handed down its book learning while the New England farm was handing down a very much greater measure of education for life. In those same years, up to the war between North and South, the Carolina plantations, weak in the transmission of literacy, none the less passed on cotton culture and the plantation crafts. And with all their gains for freedom of the spirit, as noted in my first chapter, the little New England school born on St. Helena Island in 1862, and the little Negro farms, which had their beginnings during the period of northern occupation, fell short at some points of the old order of slavery days. There was no organization to carry on ditching on a proper scale, no inspiration to gather mud and marsh grass for fertilizer, no knowledge about live stock. Yet in all life there must be constantly renewed growth or there is an end to life itself. Compared with the progressive wheat lands of the West and the truck farming which had made such strides in Virginia, the sea islands were touched by the march of agriculture only in spots. The revolution which had swept over agricultural methods, as sweeping almost as the industrial revolution in the cities, was not felt on these isolated islands.

Aunt Sophy, in the grandmothers' class.

Soon we woke up to the fact that the agriculture we had set out to teach in Penn School was not that practiced on the farms. It was a new agriculture. It was not that the transplanted school of letters fulfilled its mission less well than the New England school, nor even that the small Negro farm transmitted its heritage of the ways of soil and rain and growth less roundly than the plantation, but that there was this new body of learning and of labor which neither could transmit from the past, for neither the past of the New England school nor that of the plantation farm held it.

So it was that we came to see that if we were to serve as carriers of this new and scientific husbandry from the fenced fields and market gardens, the agricultural colleges and the government experiment stations, we must reach the fathers and mothers. Out of our work with children in the agricultural classes and on the school acres grew our work with the grown-ups. In turn it was out of this work with the parents that the children's home acres grew. There has been this interplay throughout; and, moreover, the very core of our experiment in adult education lay in engaging the participation not of factory workers in a city, nor hands on a great truck farm, but of a group of small independent farmers who must learn how to organize under their own leaders.

Our rides about the island had shown us the setting of its culture. Here was a region of low-lying land, great mud flats stretching out at low tide, tidal rivers cutting into the land and isolating still further a much-scattered people. Here was soil that could easily be built up with the fertilizer provided by nature herself in the mud and the marsh grass from the rivers, and the trash from the woods. Here was water for the digging, here were swift-growing pine and the slower oak, plenty of oyster shells for roads and for lime on the land, and oysters and sea food for the table. Even the fiddler crabs play in the island orchestra. Starvation was far from a man's elbow, but none the less easy living at a low level was not holding the oncoming generation. Young men and women were turning their backs on the opportunity which had seemed so fair in the early days of freedom. New standards of living, new goals for struggle were needed.

Our Farmers' Fair, called "De World's Fair," was the first step in the new agricultural life. The people were told to bring in their exhibits; the big hall was filled with them and then filled with the people to whom they belonged. The people themselves, with the school farmer as chairman, raised the money for the prizes and for the barbecue served at sunset. All day the big iron pot was on the fire built in the open field. A whole cow was needed for the crowd. The rice and vegetables cooked in with the beef made a very tasty dish, served with a cracker on a paper plate, the cracker being useful to help manipulate the food to the mouth. Prophet Wyne, who had come out from the farming of plantation days, was our first cook. He it was who in a later day was to comfort his neighbors with the reflection: "I feeds de boll weevil and I spect de Lord will feed me." But he lost out on that prophecy! Now the post is held by a Penn School graduate who has come through the new school of agriculture.

The fair came to stay. It exhibits in cross-section the life of the island. It has shown a steady growth in standards of living. At the early fairs, the long-staple cotton held first place, but as time went on and the crowd saw the corn, sugar cane, rice, and peas of their more progressive neighbors, the quilts and other articles which make the homes more comfortable and attractive, they realized more with every year that the one-crop farmer has the poorest chance in the long run.

I confess that our Farmers' Fairs would be of little worth if the agricultural work they dramatize stopped there. Enthusiasm is an evanescent thing when the crowd scatters and one goes back to the same old conditions and loses sight of the inspiring exhibits. "De bes' way to strike down de liar who say de Negro ain't wuk, is to show him de wuk," said an island leader at one of the fairs, but even if one went home filled with the desire to win those prizes next year, it was easy to fall into the old ruts and forget all the good talk. And much of the hard "wuk" counted for little because of worn-out soil and outworn methods.

IV

If you ever saw Seaman A. Knapp you will not forget his vivid personality. He was the inventor of a revolutionary method for teaching adults. He had been professor of agriculture, and then president of the Iowa State College. His name was widely known as writer and editor of agricultural periodicals. He had gone to Louisiana, to that section which had been settled by the Acadians described in Longfellow's "Evangeline," and which was the scene of a new sort of colonization. Immigrants from the Northwest had been invited and urged to settle there. The advertisements they had read were attractive. Many came, and many left before breakfast the next morning, discouraged completely by conditions that they found. Now Dr. Knapp had been president of the Iowa State School for the Blind five years before this happened. He must have studied a great deal on how to make blind people see.

He began with a demonstration on an acre properly handled. People could see on the land as on a map, and they began to be converted. Soon what had been swamps, prairies, and waste land were producing rice, sugar cane, corn, cotton, and live stock. Twenty years later Dr. Knapp said, "We then learned the philosophy and power of agricultural demonstration." He saw farming as a game to be played, and he knew it was a losing game unless food crops and corn could come to the South.

The boll weevil was on its way to the Atlantic Coast when Dr. Frissell, president of our board, brought Dr. Knapp to St. Helena. We had been telling the people in the churches and in the praise houses that they must raise their food, for cotton was doomed. But they would not believe. Some got a clear idea of the boll weevil's importance, however, as was shown by their notions of its size. When the news went home that there was a boll weevil at the school—it had been brought down from Washington for class work as a specimen—a terrified parent sent me a message, "I yeddy [hear] yo' has one ob dem bo' evils at de school. I pray yo' ain't let him out to eat up my chillun." After one of our meetings in a praise house a farmer said scornfully, "I ain't fearful, I stan' ober my fiel' and shoot him down jes luk a chicken hawk!" The "bo' evil" could never cross our rivers it was claimed and for the most part our islanders settled down to their cotton again.

But under the leadership of Dr. Knapp we set out to prepare for the coming of the pest and made a beginning on Penn School farm—we and the Government! A white agent visited us regularly for a year and advised us as to methods and as to alternative crops. It was a valuable experience in teaching us how the plan was worked before we began to work it ourselves! Then our school farmer was appointed as United States Farm Demonstrator, thus connecting St. Helena and the nearby islands with Washington. The men knew their records were to be reported. There was a new thrill in the work of this isolated group! And all through the years since our farm demonstrator has been a member of the Penn School family with his office on the Penn School farm.

When Dr. Knapp saw the old cornstalks planted four feet apart each way, he said, "Begin your attack right there," and right there we started. There were six farmers valiant enough to trust an acre to the new method (no, it was only a half acre that first year). Fortunately, two of them were preachers.

The Rev. D. C. Washington and the Rev. Paris Simmons were uncommon men in many ways. Both had a large following of Baptists, one in the Brick Church, the old original Baptist church of the island, where as slaves the Negroes had come and sat in the gallery; the other in Ebenezer near by. The "split" had come in the early years of their religious freedom, due to a question of choice of minister, but this was long before our day, and the early bitternesses were forgotten. Both men were island farmers. To win their enthusiasm meant much for the speed of the movement! So they were the first men approached and their half acres were watched with trembling interest by all of us. Pictures were taken of the crop, and in one "Reverend's" home today you can see an enlarged photograph in a wide gilt frame of the principal in his cornfield, where the corn waves enthusiastically far above her head. Another picture in our record book but not on the Reverend's wall, shows another field of corn planted earlier, by the old method and only half as good looking!

Then there was Robert Green, a church deacon, old enough to be the father of his teacher in the field, but not too old to learn from him. His farm has continued on the side of progress all through these years and now you will find his wife carrying on, making records in raising tomatoes and okra for the oyster factory which with time has become a canning factory. Robert has died, but in his family there is still the desire to hold on and the willingness to try the new! His son-in-law, John Henderson, is a type of the younger generation making an uphill fight against economic odds, with no thought of giving up. John's children are in Penn School so from the grandparents down there is a continuity in agricultural interest which it is the business of the school to hold.

Economics and religion go hand in hand in an agricultural community school. The Rev. D. C. Washington raised fifty-four bushels as against seventeen; the Rev. Paris Simmons doubled his crop. Fortunately every demonstration came through successfully and the preachers preached on corn, wearing a prize button sent down from Washington. The movement was young then and that button was a push button in a very real sense! Such a bit of recognition went far toward making the movement popular, as well as the fact that the crop more than doubled in the field of every demonstrator. Corn in the drill fairly beat the old method of corn in the check.

Can you see the young farmer with his agricultural training back of him—our school-teacher and government demonstrator in one, a "mere boy" to the older man he wanted to help? Into the field he went, sometimes taking the plow harnessed to the little salt marsh tackie, as the native ponies are called, and showing what he meant by close cultivation; sometimes down on his knees in the furrow beside the old farmer who followed his directions:

> One for the crow,
> And one for the mole.
> One for the rot,
> And one for you.

He dropped the kernels into the holes two feet nearer together than under the old method.

Our demonstration agent is now Benjamin Barnwell, a native-born islander whose home is on Ladies Island, just across a bit of a river and marsh which has been bridged during all of our time. As a boy he had walked to school each day and as he sat in the classroom one morning when a Hampton teacher happened to be visiting Penn she noticed him particularly and said after we had left the room, "You surely have a Hampton boy in that last row." Always alert, with eyes that glow with interest in his work, he answered the prophecy, went through Hampton, and did return to his own people. First as a farmer on the Penn School farm he put his learning to work, then he took up the demonstration work, and has carried his skills to the Negro farmers of all parts of Beaufort County.

Night work as well as day is demanded from such a teacher, for to the praise houses and the society halls he must go to explain what lies beyond the work in hand—demonstrations in soil building, in raising better cattle and poultry, and other crops besides corn. He must help them organize the ditching and help them raise the money for the new Rosenwald schools—he even helps them in improving the home and building chicken coops.

He is helping the farmers take off their dark glasses! As he goes among his own people, he goes as one who has come through their own experiences, to pass on all that he learned and is learning.

The first boll weevil year, 1919, will long be remembered. When the people woke up to find they had lost three-fourths of their crop, destroyed by that small worm in the cotton boll, one of them expressed the depth they had reached in the island phrase we had heard applied to desperate illnesses—"We sure has a satisfyin' affliction," he said. The World War had shown the ten cotton-growing states more clearly than they had ever seen before what it means to spend all your time on clothes. The South had been trying so hard to clothe the world, she had forgotten to feed herself. If the trains had been stopped, some of the southern cities could not have fed their inhabitants a week. The struggle to produce cotton, cotton, cotton, resulted in poor land, poor people, and illiteracy, and this is not a question of color! To produce $300 worth of cotton at a cost of $225 worth of food does not make farming profitable. By this time, however, our counter movement had made headway. The group of farmers who followed the lead of our pioneer preachers had records to report and the Farmers' Fairs gave it all publicity.

James Johnson talked for his group when he said at one of the fairs:

De las' time I talk fr'm dis platform, I talk 'bout Mr. Cotton, but dis time I'm goin' to talk 'bout prowision. I raise good cotton, too. De merchants kin trus' my cotton. But cotton ain't stan' no mo', an' I say, "Look yuh! Wut yo' goin' to do 'bout de animul an' de chillun?"

Fust I study 'bout de animul. Got two horse and a half to feed, so I 'cide to plant me some oats. Den I tek five task o' lan' [a task is one-fourth of an acre] an' I plow it an' I harrow it, an' I plush dat lan'. An' den it ain't suit me an' I plush um again. Den I tek bough outen de woods an' trail um ober de lan' fo' help cover de seed. An' it ain't ben long fo' I look yonder an' I see de oats sta't fo' sprout up in de fiel'.

An', my frien's, wen de time come, I cut eight wagon load off dat fiel', an' my animul, dey live on um fr'm dat day to dis!

Well, dat fix de horses, but how 'bout de chillun? I fix to plant co'n fo' de chillun. Yo' know some people tink yo' kin raise crop outen de lan'. But I tell yo' right now, you try to raise crop outen de lan' an' yo' aih't raise um mo' dan dat high. An' den de white people say yo' kin raise crop wid de fertilizer, but I cyant raise my crop dat-a-way, 'cause I cyant buy de fertilizer. But I go in de wood and I rake me trash, an' I go in de crick an' I cut me ma'sh. Hab dem long kin' of boats dat ketch me up yuh—an' I hab manure in de shed an' I pit um all on de lan'. An' I raise me a crop too! Ain't got no cotton, but I got oats fo' de horse, an' co'n and peas an' sweet potatoes fo' de chillun, an' den a few head ob hog to pit 'long wid dat.

Now de people go to Savannah an' all about fo' wuk-out money. Wuk-out money is all right, but wuk-out money's like las' night rain—run in one han' an' out de udder. I ain't got no money but I got de prowision!

"De worl' is berry lightful now, an' we mus' see whut is goin' on," said one of our progressives. "I ain't never plant till de full ob de moon," confessed another, "so I cyant plant till next week. But I'll change from de check to de drill, now I years it from yo' own lips."

This re-education of grown men and women has been at the heart of Penn School's work and with it the development of better teamwork by which they can use their knowledge collectively.

V

When you come through the rustic gate that leads from the road to Hampton House, as the principal's home on Penn School farm is called, you walk up a row of old grindstones which go far back into the lives of the people. If you come in the spring, you will see on either side flowers that can stand the hot summer sun. They grow in soil made out of the pure sand of the abandoned cotton field where Hampton House was erected in 1904. The stones and the flowers are significant of the struggle of the people in securing the necessities of life and the beauty of life, too.

The seamed surfaces of the grindstones are in truth like a phonograph record which would tell the story of the island if they could be turned with imagination. In the old plantation days a peck of corn was doled out to each family on Saturday nights. Every family had to prepare the next week's ration, if it took till "dayclean" —delicious hand-ground "grits" that "eat sweeter" than any ground by the modern power mills! The use of these old stones held on in the period following the war; and their discard registered the coming of a new day in industry and southern life. The old method, as old as Abraham, gave way.

Now as we step on the stones, we can hear in reverie the older generation singing at their grinding in the old slave streets. But that is only part of their story.

They are the only stones on this sandy island, so they were one of the few crystallizations of wealth in the hands of the people. In the day of the island's need they stood for capital and credit. A great storm in 1911 destroyed homes and crops and grim poverty had to be endured until the new crop. Penn School organized the relief work and encouraged the people to bring in their idle stones to exchange for the lumber, nails, food, or whatever was needed to tide them over. They did this with great joy; what they had they gave; so here are the old grindstones, a bit of a museum for an agricultural school, sunk in the soil itself, surely their proper setting, great rough coins of island credit.

As such they were waymarks of the beginning of a new organization—verily stepping-stones to progress in island life—for the storm led to our Coöperative Society. Never shall I forget that autumn, driving through the rough plantation roads or riding our ponies in and out among the wrecked homes. Great trees lay uprooted in the paths, all the leaves stripped off the branches. Suddenly the new leaves began to come, so that it looked like spring. "See, Missus Cooley, what de trees is doing! Dey spring forth again! Dat is what me mus' do," said Mrs. Juno, and this note of hope sounded all through that difficult winter. The first appeal that came to my office was for some vegetable seed, and the usual reply to my greeting would be, "Tanksful fo' life." There was little else they could be thankful for. "We mus' fly about like de birds w'en he rain," was all too true, for many of the homes had hardly a dry spot till repairs could be made.

The Coöperative Society was born the next spring; a little group of men meeting in the home of the school farmer, two ministers, our doctor, and five others, all island farmers who were eager to learn how to finance their own farming operations. Ireland and Denmark have helped St. Helena. Sir Horace Plunkett came on our horizon through Dr. Frissell. Both of these men, with their wide vision and experience, marked out the path of possibilities, and a more recent visit to Denmark showed me results that served as a spur to our efforts.

In plantation days, meetings among the Negroes were discouraged for there was fear of uprisings in the minds of many an overseer and these men of power did not care to see leadership develop among the slaves. As a consequence, save for the churches, there has been no tradition of teamwork among our island people. There was no training in business affairs. A first tryout in savings and credit had been a bitter experience. Their losses when the Freedmen's Bank failed drove them back to the safety of stockings and mattresses for their money. And the failure of a Beaufort bank a few years ago again tested their faith most severely. One grandmother had over $1,600 put aside for the education of her "grands." When she lost all, she came to me and said, "Now I gib yo' Abram an' Juanita. I gib um to yo' and de Lord!" You see Penn School must be a mother along with her other jobs.

Very slow to you who live in cities would seem the development of this coöperative movement among our farmers. Very cautious are the officers in making the loans. It takes strength of character to refuse your friend when he wants a loan that does not fall within the scope of the society, or to reduce the loan called for. "I know it is berry easy to borrow, but ef he bin a hard year, we has berry hard gettery! I has two or three buttons on my coat, but some men I see has but one," was the wise counsel of one of the older heads when too large a loan was asked for. "I'll jes hab to sit an' listen," said a new member when called on to speak, "I'm green now." "We'll dry yo' out soon," called out the president. As the years have come and gone, younger leaders have taken their places; coöperative buying and selling are carried on, a credit union has been organized, and a group of island farmers are shipping their potatoes, peanuts, and turkeys coöperatively.

Fortunately, as I have already pointed out, the merchants who settled on the island in the post-war years were friends of the early teachers and became friends to the people. James R. Macdonald was an outstanding example of a philanthropist in business. Together with the school, he taught the freedmen the value of home ownership. Never was he willing to mortgage the house or the land. Many a time did he argue patiently with his customer and finally refuse him the loan that would put him in danger. He was a teacher in economics to whom all the people owe a large debt of gratitude. "Him my daddy," say the old islanders as they stand in front of his picture in my office today. His successors in the business, Mark Batchelder and William Keyserling, have continued his policies, and the Corner Store and Penn School have worked as partners in the community upbuilding.

None the less, in cotton days, life went around in a never ending circle. The people planted cotton, chopped the grass, then bought feed for cattle and food for the household. The merchants loaned on the crop. The debt was paid when the cotton was sold. A new loan was taken out for the next crop. "We owed it before we growed it," said old Prince, and as he sat on our porch one autumn morning he told me he had paid every debt he owed. "How much have you left?" I asked him. "Jes' fifty cents," was the reply.

The cotton had certain advantages. Money could be seen at the end of every row. The people knew how to raise it, for it was a hand-down from generation to generation. Cash is terribly needed in rural communities and the lack of it drives the young people to the cities where it can be picked up as a less seasonable commodity. But the disadvantages loom large, too. Cotton is a robber crop, and when it is raised as the one crop it means a land and a people growing poorer. The women and the children did much of the work and their time was never counted in the cost.

The boll weevil discovered all the weak spots in the system and indirectly helped to bring in a larger freedom to the people amid all their difficulties. Unless adult education and coöperation can travel along together and keep pace with economic changes, there is little chance for the small farmer. With education he can prosecute his search for new cash crops with some chance of success in making the change; with coöperation he can contrive new advantages in handling them for market. Eight years of small beginnings we have had in our coöperative, but one can't rush a rural civilization. The Orient can teach us that, and well do we remember the visit of Daniel Swamidos to our island. He had come from India to study American educational methods for rural Negroes. He wore his turban; sometimes it was blue, sometimes white, and sometimes the delicious watermelon pink. It proved open sesame on the trains of the South, for his dark skin was just like our own people's; and when he declared that he could hardly take his eyes off Aunt Nancy because she reminded him so much of his own mother, we felt that the East and the transplanted East had indeed met together. Mr. Swamidos told us of their coöperatives in India, how the officers in some places had used a strong box buried in the earth for their bank, and yet how they had held on and come through. It helped us to have patience, to look through his eyes of vision, and to realize afresh that what others have done we can do.

And so, in turn, I will tell you about our Coöperative Society, its struggles, its near failure, its small measure of success. That little group of nine men who were the founders in 1912 went out from their meeting determined to get new members; and that first year 111 were enrolled. The average loan was $24.07, sixty-three loans were made, and ninety sacks of fertilizer were bought and sold to the members. It was a good crop year and the little society sailed through smooth waters with flags flying.

The storm that led to the birth of the society gave it its first chance to do some coöperative work for the community. Our main road was in terrible condition. The county had hauled oyster shells for its repair, and a great pile lay at the edge of the tide river near the school. There they stayed for over a year, while the island people and horses were "punished" by the poor road. This was the day before automobiles, and roads were made by the simple method of dumping shells along the way to be broken down by the carts and other vehicles. A simple system but a very perfect road resulted after an incredibly short time of discomfort.

The officers of the society saw their chance. When work was slack, the call went out, and men with their oxen, ponies, and carts responded. The merchants also helped, and in a few days our road was in good shape. This experience welded membership. It also showed who were the weak reeds in the society for not quite half of them came out for this volunteer service. Those who worked came from a great variety of plantations, from Land's End to Coffins Point, the far ends of the island.

Then came ditching, another opportunity for coöperation and a much more difficult one. One of the difficulties of rural life is that necessities crowd one upon another. As I look back, it is clear that we should always
have done a great deal more in keeping up the organized ditching. In slavery days this had been a regular
part of the year's work. They tell me of miles of shining ditches, glistening in the sunlight with the wild
flowers growing along the banks. The drivers had the
necessary "hands" to put at the task; the cotton crop
depended upon the ditches being kept open; it was all
in the day's work. But with the division of the plantations into small holdings, there was no organization to
carry on. If a man did dig the ditch on his own little
farm, what good did it do if his neighbor did not dig
his; and there were the main trunks, the large ditches
which seemed to belong to nobody, and into which all
the small ditches ran; miles and miles of ditches, all in
bad shape through neglect.

Ditching was much discussed at our early fairs, but
nothing came of it. It remained for the Coöperative Society to set things going; and soon we were all deep in
ditches! We who were standing back of the society
took our share in inspecting, and encouraging and urg-
ing! Fourteen miles were actually cleared. The merchants coöperated. The Department of Agriculture at
Washington sent us an expert to go over the old ditches
and give us advice on any needed changes. No changes
were advised, showing the agricultural knowledge of
the old planters. Finally through the efforts of the
county commissioners, with William Keyserling, one
of our island merchants, as chairman, a one-mill tax
was added for the St. Helena district for ditching pur-
poses. As the total was not enough to cover the ex-

pense, the two firms on the island contributed $100 each, the work was put in charge of our superintendent and the school contributed his planning and supervision. The final report given at the Farmer's Fair was twenty-eight miles dug and cleaned on twenty-five plantations. The record in malaria went down as the record in crops came up! And we are holding our own on that enemy of the slaves and the planters in the old days.

Crops did go up! At the Fair that fall one of the older farmers had his chance to speak. He had been most unwilling to join in the ditching outside of his own land. Finally he had to be fairly forced to do it. He now told how he had been able to pay his debt of $200 on his house, $90 at the store, $30 at the school where he had his buggy repaired, and then put some money in the bank. It had been a good year for him! But not a word did he say about the ditches. That was a delicate subject! As he walked down the aisle, someone in the audience called out, "What about those ditches?" He paused before he said with a twinkle in his shining black eyes, "Dem ditches ain't do one bit of harm to my lan.'"

By 1918 the society had handled $13,865.44 and, with all the experiences gained, had $58.00 out in bad debts. Year by year, if we could read between the lines of its minute book, we should see the honest efforts to hold on, the difficulties met. The meetings were full of interest to all of us. I heard one of the officers say, "We must stop excusing ourselves by saying the Lord sends the rain! The Lord gives us brains and strong arms for the ditching! We say the Lord sent the drought! He gives us brains and strong arms to save every drop of moisture by cultivating right." "Stop raising nubbins!

Stop being a nubbin!" was the vigorous advice of one who had paid his loan with interest promptly. One of the men who had borrowed $15 was found out as a double dealer; he had mortgaged his cow to the merchant, the same cow to the society. A committee of two was sent out "to visit him and teach him," one of them saying as he took on the job, "Things have been raggy. We members have been raggy too in our coming and going." Nine members were dismissed at one meeting because they would not meet their obligation and pay the eighty-one cents each member was taxed to cover the loans unpaid because of death or inability to collect. The total liability clause in the constitution (all the members being liable for all the loans) has worked well in keeping the society healthy and afloat. It is in the back of their minds, even if it has had to be put into practice but once.

The "Bold Evil" tested the society to its marrow. If he did not prove his magnitude, the vast numbers of his family descending on our cotton fields demonstrated that "in union there is strength." Could our little co-operative make headway against the scourge by the application of the same principle? The old sea-island long-staple cotton for which the region is famous seems to be beaten by the weevil. It is blighted before it is ready to gather. Early maturing seed has made the short staple a possibility. Young demonstrators are using improved seed and improved cultural methods and unless the season is entirely on the side of the weevil, cotton has its chance. But it must take its place alongside the other crops. The struggle is on, and conditions hold a threat which serves as a spur to the young.

New crops were advised. Peanuts took first place,

promised well, and then the prices went down! Rice
had its advocates; whoever has eaten South Carolina
rice, and especially ours on the island, knows it is the
best! Loans were made on the basis of the new crops
and acres were visited by the Committee of Management. "Momently and hourly I love this Society and
my mind is open to it," said one of the farmers in the
field. In our enthusiasm the society put a part of its
capital into a rice thresher. That was a proud day when
the members went out to see it work! It was a miracle!
The Committee of Management expected acres of rice
to be harvested, brought to the machine, and then sold
coöperatively. A great step seemed to have been taken.
But that second miracle has never happened! Very few
of our island families have used it and it has proved a
poor investment, except as the school and a few members have reaped the benefit. Why? Perhaps the society
tried to go too fast! Peanuts fared better, and the members have shipped coöperatively with varying degrees
of success.

In 1924 the St. Helena Credit Union was born, an
outgrowth of the Coöperative, the same membership
practically, as the "Co-ops" voted to move into the new
society as a whole. Here a new element entered—share-
holding—and each member bought a $5.00 share. It
also made it possible for members to save through their
own society, but that miracle hasn't happened either,
for a Beaufort bank failure shook the confidence of
these young Negroes as well as the older ones; if the
white men with all their business experience could not
succeed in their financial business, it looked as if the
colored men had better watch their step. This is only
a passing condition, I believe, and the Credit Union
will eventually be functioning as it should in a rounded

way. As it is, all the loans are now in the hands of the
Union, and all the buying and selling in the hands of the
"Co-ops."

Our experience with white potatoes in 1927 taught
us further lessons. The profits of large planters on the
mainland the year before led the whole county, white
and black alike, to believe the salvation of every farmer
lay in white potatoes! Everyone wanted to go into it!
And almost everyone did! On the island our Credit
Union stood behind its members and larger loans were
made to make the new crop possible. Instead of the
hoped-for $4.00 to $5.00 per barrel, the barrels themselves could not be paid for, nor the fertilizer in many
cases. The crop was grown, the barrels ready to ship,
when the market failed. The Florida crop, delayed by
a great storm, reached the northern market just
ahead of the South Carolina potatoes. When I tell you
that some of the young white women in Beaufort said
they did not want to be away from home in the evenings when their husbands returned during that period
of business collapse, you will see how the whole county
was struck. The district has not yet recovered. And our
Credit Union? It still survives, and its members hold
together. But only the interest on the loans can be paid
till we get out of the woods, or perhaps I should say,
out of the potato patch! The capital is in the hands and
held on the honor of its members.

The next chapter to be written in a few years will be
the most interesting of all. It will tell how the men
rallied, for the rally has begun! It will tell what such a
coöperative organization can do for a group of rural
Negroes—the first Negroes in the country and the
first of any group in South Carolina to organize a credit

union,—what it can do to help keep them from going under.

At our last meeting one of the men who had been sitting very quietly while the other men spoke, finally rose to his feet. This is what he said:

I ben discourage dis year. I sure ben discourage! But I ruther miss somet'ing else dan dis meeting! An' now I meet wid some good farmers I feel boom up!

I los' on cotton, couldn't pay fo' de fertilizer. I mek prowision or I'd have had to lef' here. I feel oneasy, but ef this society will give me my chance, I'll try to come out.

The society with all its ups and downs is a part, and a most vital part, of our work for the grown-ups.

VI

On my first trip to the sea islands years ago, I had seen the truck gardens about Norfolk, an omen of the new days in the coastal plains of the Carolinas. Beginnings even then had been made about Beaufort, our county seat on Port Royal Island. Would these people on the nearby islands, I asked myself, be able to hold their lands? Would the land be able to hold them?

Often in those days we would stop a young fellow driving an oxcart and ask him what he had been doing since he left school. Usually the answer would be, "Nuttin'," and with a few more questions we would find that he was busy on the home farm. One morning when we met Roachie on the road with his cart full of marsh grass, I asked the usual question and received the usual answer. Even when caught with the goods, farming was "Nuttin.' "

It is no wonder that Roachie skipped "off island"

when his first opportunity came. That family numbered nine and the father was ill. The mother has spent much of her time at the oyster factory, where she earned about twenty cents a day shucking oysters brought up the little tide rivers in the oyster boats. A beautiful picture they make as they creep in at sunset time, sometimes the rowers singing as they swing along; but a dreary picture it is when you follow their cargoes through the factory and see the women and girls standing in the wet as they shuck all day and receive a pittance at the end of it for the cans they turn in.

Roachie's family raised enough sweet potatoes to carry them through the year, and enough grits and peas, but when the taxes were paid and the church and society dues, there was little left to make home attractive to a bunch of growing boys and girls; no chance to build the new rooms needed to give them privacy and comfort. So the drift away came very easily, for a change could hardly be for the worse and they heard of the gold and good times in the city.

Here on this little island of black people a man is a man who owns his own acres. And a love for the land has been inherited too, a love which wells up when it comes to a question of selling. There are only a few white people on the island and between the two races there has always existed the friendliest sort of feeling. Here the Negro can prove the stuff that is in him. But a motive for life is needed. There is gold in the land too, if only they know how to get it. Through the school and through our community work we have sought to build up new aspirations to give that self-reliant incentive which will take the place of the old lash of slavery.

On the one hand, this must come from within and only those will survive who attain it. There is no real

Uncle Sam, at eighty-eight an enthusiastic farmer.

fear of starvation on the island; the county schools are improving every year; the roads are better and people can get about more easily. New tools, new crops, new markets are ready to hand; new wants are coming thick and fast as life broadens beyond the edges of the islands.

On the other hand, factors outside the control of school or islanders press in and condition the outcome. In their search for new money crops, will these self-dependent Negro farmers be driven to the wall? Not only has the boll weevil changed the economic situation, but taxation, which bears unequally on the small landowners, has become a heavy burden at a time when the struggle is at its height. A bridge has been built between Beaufort and Ladies Island, linking St. Helena with the mainland, a bridge which may prove to be a blessing or a curse to the people. "Good roads make a nation great," said Robert Bacon many years ago. But there must be an equalization between the cost and the means for paying the bill. If automobiles and the pleasure of tourists are the main objects to be considered, as seemed the case in some of the early projects, this Negro community can only grit its teeth and make the best possible struggle to show it can hold on till it is taxed so far beyond the limit of its earning power, that the holding on is no longer in the strength of its own hands. That is one jaw of the pincers.

The other is the encroachment of large-scale mechanized farming. Under the old cotton régime, there was little danger of losing the land, for the Negroes hold in small tracts not practical for cotton culture in the hands of planters. Now that trucking has come into the picture, the smaller acreage can be used and is wanted. Lands that are forfeited because of back taxes are picked up. The temptation to sell the old birthrights presents itself in cash offers that seem large to people who see little money in the course of the year and are untutored as to the difference between income and capitalization.

It hangs in the balance whether the forces for education and coöperation among the islanders will develop mutual strength among them swiftly enough to outflank this tendency toward dispossession; swiftly enough to enable a countryside of small growers to hold their own by using modern methods of cultivation and by handling their products in common as the small farmers of Denmark, Ireland, and Belgium have done through their coöperative associations. Otherwise, the clock will turn back; and another generation will see the individual farms which, with emancipation, took the place of the old plantations, themselves succeeded by great truck farms—a mess of pottage in a modern guise. Under such a régime huge tracts would be worked by seasonal labor on seasonal wages and the descendants of the old slaves would lose their foothold on the soil; and with it their brief tenure of racial self-dependence and all that it means.

This is the challenge that confronts the younger generation on St. Helena. They must use the talents buried in the old deeds. They must meet the economic change with the new skills of agriculture, the new team plays of collective effort. That negative "nuttin'" has had to be changed to a positive. Ranking agriculture with letters in the school has helped. Organizing the farm life in the community has helped. But the thing that has been basic has been the eager spirit of the people themselves. Where Penn School has touched the grown folks has counted for a difficult present, but where it has helped unfold the nascent capacities of the young folks, as they have entered into the set-up of land and labor—there it has counted for the future. There we feel that the old Penn School bell has proclaimed a new liberty.

Let me put it in terms of homely experience and youthful adventure. When Kermit graduated he could either "hunt job" in the city or go back to the land on Ladies Island and to that home which his mother had been able to keep together while she sent three children to school. First came a few months in Savannah which showed him that there were too many others "hunting job," and then, the wiser for his experience, he returned to carry on where there was plenty of work though a discouraging lack of ready money. In addition to the farm activities there was the porch to renew, the house to whitewash and paint. Through his efforts a Young Peoples Union came into being, and he was soon up to his elbows in that. Not only did they have meetings for election of officers and talk; they helped raise the money for the new Rosenwald School that the community was bending every nerve to secure; helped spread books from the school library.

Follow other young men out on to the plantations. There is Tony Jones who was never able to finish school but who has kept up with the "Co-ops" and the Credit Union, and who has held on in spite of a fire in his little shop where he made some of the cash so longed for and so limited in our island group. Fred Fripp, too, has landownership first in his economics, and has bought a tract of forty acres, nearer the school than his father's land, a part of which he will inherit. Fred walked his eighteen miles a day when he attended Penn School; then came a long struggle when he put himself through Hampton; then a new chance came at

Penn when the spread of invention brought automobiles and engines to school. He is in charge of our power plant. His first savings went into the land and into the home for his family. As a young leader he was able to form a company of men on his old plantation and together they secured a tract of woods where they can hunt to their heart's content. (Much of our waste land is held in private preserves by northern or southern whites, and to these the resident Negroes are usually not admitted.) There they hope in the future to develop their own playground. This sort of thing counts tremendously in giving lure to a farming community. When years ago, as a boy, George Brown decided that Savannah would give him a larger chance to earn his clothes and other much desired pleasures, he left school. But his mother hunted him up and there was a real though friendly battle between mother and son. "Mrs. Virginia," herself a graduate of the old Penn School, won; and now on the acres which George has bought with his own earnings you will find the group of little Browns—there are eight of them now—and all of them from the grandfather to the new baby are in the Penn School "family."

The young farmers are the ones who carry the annual Farmers' Fair. They not only organize it, but through their own enthusiasm pass on to their neighbors the urge for better things. They are to be seen examining the exhibits brought in, comparing their own, listening to others, explaining to some, and when the time comes for the farmers' talks, they give their experiences so that all may know how they have come along their journey that crop year. They are using the school library; taking part in regular community sings, the irregular entertainments, and the regular Parents' Association. From that far-away neighborhood on Ladies Island where Kermit lives there comes a large group to see the Christmas Mystery. To the school they travel back from the most remote corners when tools are to be replaced or a harvest problem to be talked out with their leaders. Practically every day in one way or another they are "hit" by the school. The school workers, in automobiles, in the buckboard, and on pony back make daily connections, and so the circle of contacts keeps up like the chain of an "all hands round."

These young farmers belong to the new day. They have learned to grow corn, to grow peanuts, to grow more and better chickens and pigs. They are learning how to make farming an all-year job, though most of them have to piece it out with work at their trades or wages at a factory for a part of the season. The conservatism of the older farmers is giving way to the eagerness of the younger men who stand beside them. The ditches are being dug! The "Co-op" and the Credit Union are determined to meet the challenge. There is an increasing group loyalty as there is an expanding experience in team play.

Never in the history of these sea islands has there been so great a need for a school with an all-year-round program that tries to fit into the whole community life. The larger tools and ways are necessary. We have come from harness mended with string to automobiles; from the ox to the tractor; and the young people who have felt the pull both ways, the temptation to go to the cities and the call to the land, and who are giving of their best in local leadership are the hope of the island today. The fathers found it hard to make changes; the sons are making them and their sons will be still better fitted to cope with the new.

PART V

THINGS OF THE SPIRIT

I

ONE spring we took long drives about the island with a skilled photographer from Hampton Institute, and with lines from Sidney Lanier in our notebooks. Whenever we came upon a scene of tidal river or moss-hung oaks that fitted "The Marshes of Glynn," the camera caught and made prize of it. Even more easily can local habitations be given to texts from the Old and New Testaments.

To one brought up on the Bible there are everywhere suggestions of life and labor in Judea. The cotton pickers bending in the rows, their simple lives close to the soil, take the place of the workers in the vineyard. For the shepherds in the fields, there are the boys and sometimes the older women who drive in the cattle or the turkeys. Here are the oxen, small to be sure, like our marsh "tackies," but still used on the roads and in the fields. There are the fishermen, coming in on the tide after dark. Or perhaps of a morning you may see Uncle Sam standing up in his boat with his net held in his mouth, ready to cast far out on the water with his hand—a silhouette against the sky, performing an act of life that is timeless. Well might St. Peter have cast in the same way. The vocations of the Twelve Apostles, with the exception of Matthew the money changer, could be drawn from the island life with very little change.

All this is more than a physical resemblance. A religious imagery overlays fields and roads and tidal rivers. The life of the spirit walks among the Negro people. Abraham and the prophets are more real to them than the old slave owners who gave their names to the plantations. The Bible heroes live in the imagination of the people like the great oak on the road to Coffins Point. The big wind seems to many of them as the direct Breath of God; the thunder as God's voice. To come on cool air in a wood shows that the spirits have just been there. Perhaps it was not unnatural for Dan, who had never seen a picture before, to gaze intently at a photograph of the Lion of Lucerne, and ask timidly, "Is it an angel, muh?" When the great zeppelin, the Los Angeles, flew over the island one day, the teachers sent the children out so they should not miss seeing it. Many were heard exclaiming as they looked up into the sky, "Where is dat lost angel?" Angels seem nearer to many sea-island children than lions and zeppelins! The minister who prayed for the school as "de bridge over de Red Sea into de Promised Land fo' we people, de pillar of cloud by day and de pillar of fire by night," was using a language perfectly understood by his hearers. Here as in few of our cities today can a speaker have confidence that every biblical allusion will be caught by his hearers.

We find a dignity and simplicity among young and old in meeting death, which is due to their religion. The reality to them of the Golden Gates and the Starry Crown gives courage and they talk of approaching death as few white people would dream of doing. When I visited a little child who seemed to be dying I offered her the soup she had refused. To arouse her I asked, "Who is giving you the soup, Lilly?" "Jesus Christ is feeding me," was the unexpected reply, unexpected to me but perfectly natural to the island parents who interpreted it as a sign that the child was ready to die.

All this is so because the Bible for years was the one book in the island homes and because of the strong

Fred Fripp, who walked eighteen miles a day for his education at Penn.
Now a father making a Better Home.

religious bent of the Negro. Whatever may be the result on the race of changing conditions, however far
away from the faith of their fathers the young race of
today may seem to be straying, there is something
fundamental in their religious inheritance, something
strong and elemental that should not be allowed to be
destroyed.

II

There was one saying of the Master they bear alle-
giance to in freedom, which was well-nigh forgotten,
so it seemed to us, when we first visited among the
people. "Unless ye become as little children." Perhaps
there had been no rendering of that text under slavery
that caught its meaning for boys and girls. The Negro
child of the sea islands knew work far better than play.
Often the first world he saw was the cotton field, for
the baby was taken to the field and left in one of the
rows to laugh or cry as the case might be, his bright
brown eyes growing accustomed to the cotton or the
corn, the hoe or the old ox, even before they knew the
usual household furniture. His first playthings were
the cotton stalks or grasses. Even at four he was considered old enough to help, as he could drop the cotton-
seed in the hole made by a hoe going on ahead, and
covered by a hoe or by the feet of the older person following.

Acres of cotton were still planted in this way when
we came to the island. It was as vital to introduce good,
hard play as it was to bring the farms to school or to
recapture the farmers' trades. The dignity of work had
to be paralleled with the relaxation of play. That in
truth was a neglected but joyous branch to "hang on de

wings ob dis school." And this may be the place to underscore that an agricultural school cannot lose sight of the cultural and recreational elements of education; their neglect would make for a lopsided community, and one with little appeal to young people.

We began on baseball, and our Hampton teachers were engaged to play with the pupils as well as to work with them. "I don't care how hard I work," wrote one of the boys when I was "off island." "I have a baseball game behind me, and I have a baseball game before me on Saturday." Rules and good sport spirit soon took their proper place and quarrels fell off. Basketball has been introduced. One youngster wrote, "We girls plays ball, but not feet ball!" But the boys do.

For the younger children swings and teeter boards came in the grove. They were to be heard in the early morning waiting their turns, for two swings and two teeters could hardly serve the crowd of over a hundred little girls. None had been provided for the boys and they stood on the outskirts, as hungry as any bread line! Later they made a swing-teeter combination in the shop which was placed on their own playground and boys were sometimes seen kicking their heels up against the starry sky as they would come to swing of an evening.

These playthings were worn out in an incredibly short time. Swings made of rope hung to the trees lasted about a week! Teeters wore through although strong oak had been used. Was ever playground apparatus so thoroughly used, we wondered. The committee devised a new plan. New swings were made of iron chains and the standard sunk in concrete. The impatient youngsters used the swings too soon; the standard was soon flat on the ground. Again it was placed in a concrete base and this time the children kept off till it set. The standard still stands, but the iron chains and the seats are constantly wearing out.

Self-initiative has made itself felt in their play. Small barefooted boys with an old piece of board for a bat and gray moss wound about the catchers hand for a glove have taken the place of knots of boys pitching into themselves on the way to school in their need for letting off physical energy. I can see with my mind's eye as I write boys and girls trundling old iron hoops taken from barrels that have brought some second-hand clothing for our sales house. Some of them had trudged five miles to school that morning I came upon them, but they showed the spring spirit as they flew after their hoops on the school roads all the recess period.

Our singing and our playing go together. Singing is as natural as breathing to the islanders; it belongs with our bright sunshine, with the long stretches of sky and clouds, with the vivid colors of marsh and river. Folk games were introduced and we often meet groups of children engaged in them on the road as they sing the melodies. Their innate sense of rhythm was well illustrated when the instruments came down for a Penn School Band. One of our Hampton teachers had been in the Hampton Band. With that experience and a correspondence course he became our band leader and in two months, after the eleven instruments had been put into the hands of eleven boys, they gave a concert! The band took its place in our curriculum of work and play. And now a harmonica band has been organized.

Our singing and our working go together—but this we did not have to teach. It is easier to chop wood to the rhythm of an old spiritual; it is easier to scrub and wash as you sing;

Ebery time I feels de sperit
Movin' in-a muh heart,
I will pray.
Oh, ebery time I feels de sperit
Movin' in-a muh heart
I will pray.
I look all around me
It look so shine,
I ask muh Lord
Ef all were mine.

More than one visitor from Africa—and we have a
steady stream of missionary leaders and government
officials who come to Penn to study our scheme of education—has been reminded of African boat songs as he
listened to the island spirituals. Perhaps this is a clue to
the southern Negro's habit of singing at work. On St.
Helena we have always sung the spirituals in the
homes, in the churches and praise houses, at the school,
and even in the whistling contest at our Junior Farmers' Fair the prizes are won on the clear and true whistling of some chosen spiritual.

Our Folk Lore Society with its occasional meetings
and the St. Helena Quartette share the responsibility
for seeing to it that these songs of the people are preserved in the midst of a faster life epitomized by the
automobiles and tractors. Natalie Curtis Burlin spent
a few weeks here before her untimely death collecting
and writing the spirituals that belong particularly to
the sea islands. These were published later in her
"Negro Folk Songs." Her death interrupted garnerings
which were deeply appreciated by all of us; but another
musician found the way to St. Helena, this time a native African from Sierra Leone, Nicholas George Julius
Ballanta, who was making a study of Negro music on
both continents. He had been assisted in securing his

musical education through the interest of George Fos-
ter Peabody, honorary president of the Penn School
Board, who has long realized that the artistic genius
of the Negro race could serve as an important contribution to our American life. One hundred and three
spirituals were recorded by Mr. Ballanta in the short
three weeks he could spend with us—but the islanders
themselves are now awake to the necessity for holding
onto these fugitive melodies, and we teachers value
them in addition as a unique educational influence.

Once every year—and that time is chosen to light up
the long pull of our real winter months when the going
is the most difficult—there is one whole delirious week
of song, which is opened by sermons on song given in
our churches. Every day at noon a concert is arranged
for chapel. Different organizations sing, the older
people as well as the younger, not only spirituals but
the folk songs of other peoples and national hymns.
The church choirs give special music of their own
choosing, and there is the quartet contest—when every
grade in the school competes for recognition as "The
Winning Quartet."

I can but wonder if it is not literally true that their
love of singing is what has carried these people through
all their experiences without bitterness.

III

Sometimes I think no one has felt the real joy of
Christmas who has not spent it at Penn School! Here
for twenty-five years we have been awakened before
"dayclean" (as the islanders call sunrise) by the singing of the old Christmas carols in our hall. Our front

door key is "stolen" the night before, a mere matter of form really, for we never lock our doors and windows on the island! The singers steal in so that we hear nothing until the glad carol bursts forth, and we realize that the gift is ours again. They steal out as quietly as they enter and we hear them go from building to building, singing. Those liquid notes in the dark of the morning usher in the Christmas week and strike the keynote for all that is to follow.

Christmas on the old plantations was the most joyful time in the whole year. It meant freedom from the routine of work, the giving out of the new clothing, more food, and drink, and on most plantations a "Christmas Gif'" for each slave; a time to mingle; a time for dance and song; the drab year gave up some sunshine when Christmas came!

And Christmas on St. Helena today keeps all that is best in the old tradition. There is no one-day limit! There is the school Christmas when all the pupils gather for the Christmas tree in Darrah Hall. Each class sings a carol as its joint gift to the holiday; everyone tries to bring something for the poorer folk; and these gifts, from one box of matches to a large bag of grits or potatoes, are laid on the benches below the tree before the excitement of receiving presents begins.

One of the classes gave a special offering last year in line with an old Moravian custom. They came into the Hall, which is darkened to give full glory to the tree with its clusters of electric bulbs. They came singing and each one carried a tallow candle fastened into an apple. White children in the North had sent down the candles and money for the apples as their share in our Christmas. I wish they could have seen the march and then heard the carol as the group faced the school.

The children sang, on and on, while the candles they carried flickered in rhythm with the song. As I looked down the row, for I stood near the tree to see that no flame came too near its branches, I saw one apple with a huge bite taken out of it. I could not but admire the initiative of the boy who tested that apple, but I admired all the more the self-control of the rest who were singing their hearts out and waiting for the future joy their candleholders held! Then came the march to the far end of the hall, candles still shining brightly and voices still caroling!

The school Santa Claus has a gift for each pupil, some candy and an orange, but perhaps none of the young folk get quite the thrill of the older members of our community class who make their curtsies and murmur "T'ank yo', Sir!" as they pass in rather solemn procession. The great day ends and hundreds of people are brought nearer to the great Christ spirit. During the week boys and girls go out to homes where provision for the holiday has been meager or perhaps none at all! They carry the gifts that were brought in by the school children and they sing the Christmas songs. They get from it more than those who receive the gifts.

And Christmas goes right on! There are the celebrations in the homes, and few homes are too poor to provide the extra treat for Christmas! There are the parties for the older boys and girls who have left the island and come home for the great week. And in the churches there are the Christmas programs. Costumes are borrowed, and "The Little Mystery" is given, a short version of the "Great Mystery" which they see at the school every other year. One year the shepherds followed a moving star the full length of the church. The stable, the Wise Men, Mary and the Christ Child, spirituals, carols, all make us realize the reality of Christmas on St. Helena. They have literally made the Mystery their own.

And "The Great Mystery Play" which comes as the climax! How shall I describe it! In our large hall where the great rafters and rough finish exactly fit the play, some sixty players, teacher, and boys and girls give the Christmas story. Even a cold night and the dark of the moon do not keep the people in their homes, for it has become a tradition and each year makes it dearer to the hearts of the island folk. Meeting Aunt Maria one morning just before Christmas, I called out, "Are you coming to the Mystery Play?" "Oh, yes!" was the reply. "I ain't neber want to miss de Mystery Play! Among all de doin's up at de school, dat Mystery ben my favorite! Hit so solemn!"

Well do I remember the first year it was given. We had brought the outline, and costumes had been donated. The boys and girls themselves probably did not understand it very well. It is easy to take too much for granted and when the night came, we found we had not explained enough. When the audience saw their own teachers and children dressed in so strange a fashion, there were little giggles all over the hall. When the angels came on the stage, that was too much! Nervousness and general excitement prevailed and rather spoiled the effect!

The next year a picture in words was given before the play began. They were all to remember they were far away in Christ's country, and they were to remember that they were seeing the pictures of the Christ Child's birth. They were to forget their children and teachers and think only of the Story. That year there was not a sound during all the scenes. "Hit so solemn."

Old English carols sung, one after another, from behind a screen which figures as the Inn and for the general background, opens the Mystery. As the last one is sung a troup of boys and girls, the minstrels and maids, come on; the boys carrying a cross made of oak and the girls swinging their wreaths made of gray moss intertwined with the cassina, which we call the Christmas berry down here. The girls are dressed in white, with broad sashes of brilliant red, and the boys have red tunics with green trimmings. They sing with great abandon,

> From far away, we come to you
> To sing of great tidings, strange and true,
> From far away, we come to you
> To sing of great tidings, strange and true.

Next they recite in unison, "Come, ye gentles, hear the story," giving the setting for all that is to follow.

As they troup off, from the other side of the stage enter a group of older women, the mourning Israelites, who sing as they kneel in prayer,

> Draw nigh, draw nigh, Immanuel,
> And ransom captive Israel,
> That mourns in lonely exile here,
> Until the Son of God appear.
> Rejoice! Rejoice! Immanuel
> Shall come to Thee, O Israel.
>
> Draw nigh, draw nigh, O morning Star
> And bring us comfort from afar.

In the center is Mary, her blue robe a lovely contrast to the dull reds of the others, brightened here and there by a few in golden yellow or soft green. They go out, singing their prayer, leaving Mary. To her the angel

Gabriel appears and gives his message. Elizabeth enters and hears the glorious news as Mary recites the Magnificat. So the first scene ends.

It is evening. The stage is darkened. Joseph and Mary come to the Inn. As Mary drops down wearily, with her bundle beside her, Joseph knocks at the Inn door only to find there is no room for them. There is a low sigh in our audience for they understand the refusal. Their eyes follow Mary and Joseph to the stable as a voice sings from behind the stage the old carol, "No room within the dwelling."

The shepherds come on. They talk quietly about the strangeness of the night, as they stretch themselves out in the "field" in the early moonlight. (Yes, we have electric lights, red, blue, and white, so color effects on our stage are made possible.) The night grows black. Something is wrong with their herds. Their fear as Gabriel appears to them, followed by the other angels, does not seem like acting at all. The voices of the unseen choir sing,

> Dere's a star in de east,
> On Christmas morn,
> Rise up shepherds, an' follow,
> It'll lead yo' to de place
> Where de Savior is born,
> Rise up shepherds, an' follow.

They go out toward Bethlehem.

After a moment's perfect stillness, voices from the far door of the hall are heard singing, "We, three kings of Orient are." In all their magnificence, down the aisle, right through the midst of the audience, our Three Kings bear their gifts "from afar." They cross the stage to the manger above which, since the search of the shepherds, swings a brilliant star. A soft light, cast upon Mary's face from the basket cradle, makes the scene fairly breath taking.

The last scene of all brings all the players on the stage, and as they sing,

> Oh, come all ye faithful, joyful and triumphant,
> O come ye, O come ye to Bethlehem

the audience feels the call of the old "Adeste Fidelis," and one can hear a soft humming in response. Then the players come down the aisles, singing the spiritual,

> Go tell it on the mountains,
> Over the hills and ebery where
> Go tell it on de mountains
> That Jesus Christ is a-born.

Finally they take their places in front of the audience in tableau, a riot of soft colors, a group of eastern people who seem to have come out of the long past.

There is no elaborate staging nor costumes. The soft clinging cheesecloth is dyed by the girls themselves. The three kings are clothed in some of the treasures sent down in the "barrels" of second-hand goods for our sales house and rifled by our vigilant Committee on Costumes. An old piano cover is now doing beautiful service on the back of the tallest king!

After these many years, the Mystery no longer seems like an importation. It seems to flow from the life of the people, as naïvely as the Passion Play given by the peasants of Oberammergau, or as we can imagine the mysteries played in medieval England. The same parts are taken by the same people year after year, till the audience would feel a shock were a different player to be substituted. Joseph and the Innkeeper, Ga-

briel, Mary, many of the mourning Israelites and shepherds and kings, yes, and the angels too! have lost their
everyday personalities for an evening. The blending of
their spirituals with the English carols, the rude stage
of Darrah Hall, the palmettoes and gray moss used in
the staging, the use of Holy Writ and simple conversation, all go together to fit our Mystery into the native
imagination of players and people.

IV

In our praise houses is found the simplest, the most
real form of the Christian religion I have ever seen.
That is the background which makes the Christmas
Mystery a natural outflowering of the community life.
On every one of the old plantations you will come
across a tiny building furnished with rude backless
benches and a leader's stand in front. The men and
women who are acknowledged as religious leaders usually sit facing the others, and their rank does not depend upon the amount of education they may have, but
on their religious fervor. The praise house leader is a
man of position and receives his appointment from the
church. He is in charge of the regular services held in
each praise house on Tuesday, Thursday, and Sunday
nights every week. These houses on the plantations
are near to hand and the people can drop in as familiarly
as they do at home. It is not so easy to travel over
country roads in the dark and so our people use their
churches only for the midday Sunday services.

The informality and simplicity of a praise house
service is gripping. Men and women, boys and girls
wander in, and take their seats, often wearing their

THINGS OF THE SPIRIT

overalls and work clothes. The only light is a small lamp on the leader's desk, and often I have seen that used without a chimney, reminding me of those lines in Julia Ward Howe's "Battle Hymn of the Republic";

I have seen Him in the watch-fires of a hundred circling
    camps;
They have builded Him an altar in the evening dews and
    damps;
I can read His righteous sentence by the dim and flaring
    lamps,
His day is marching on.

Here are sung the spirituals unchanged; here is the Scripture read as a lesson to the plantation family, here are prayers offered that show the poetic power of the race. "Pray on de knees ob yo' heart," is advised by the leader. One of the old "Mothers" prays, "May de bird ob love be in muh heart an' de Lamb ob Christ in muh bosom, an' oh, God, who tuk up de sun in de palm ob yo' han' an' t'rowed her out into de sky to be Queen ob de day, Listen to we." All through her prayer is heard the soft murmur of the response struck in the hearts of her hearers. A musical rhythm it makes, which finally breaks forth into the singing of a spiritual as the prayer comes to a close; the voice of the "Mother" on her knees mingling with the singing which grows in power as the Amen is said. Yes, the pictures are vivid and real as we listen to the older folk in their prayers; "Now as we bend our hearts equal to our knees, Lord Jesus, wilt Thou climb up on dat milk-white steed called 'Victory,' an' ride ober de mountains and t'rough de valleys of our sins an' backslidin's."

Young as well as old have their parts. In one praise house I found the young people seated together forming a choir which sang with rare beauty. Often a young boy is called on to "line off" the hymn. Those who have recently been received into the church are given this honor and are even allowed to pray or pronounce the benediction. One thinks of the Christ in the crowd, saying "A little child shall lead them," when the small congregation turns toward the East and the boy's voice is heard asking the blessing. Surely there is a hint here for all educators. That power within the youth, expressed by his "coming through" to his baptism and reception into the church, is caught by the elders before it has evaporated!

When the meeting breaks up, perhaps the old spiritual is sung;

Oh, muh sister [or it may be "muh brudder"] did yo' come fo'
    to help me,
Oh, muh sister, did yo' come fo' to help me,
Oh, muh sister, did yo' come fo' to help me,
Pray gib me yo' right hand.

From one to the other they go shaking hands in rhythm with the singing, and then the little groups wander off home through the plantation paths.

"Shouts" are occasionally held in the praise houses. They grow less frequent as the years pass and more secular entertainment is introduced in the island life. Evidently these were a link with the old African days, changed in America, to fit into the new religious life they adopted so promptly. The "Shouts" come after the service. The singers take their places on the floor, and to a rhythm that seems to rock the little house a group will begin to make those steps which belong to the Negro race. They are made always in a circle, always a group of women—or of men, but never a mixed group —and always kept up till near exhaustion; never allowed to be altered by the dance steps learned by the present generation who may go "off island" for a season. The watchful leader sees to it that no one "crosses de foot"—for that savors too much of the worldly dance.

For a people who had no play or entertainments in their lives, this was a valuable custom, for it closely connected the young people, as well as their fathers and mothers, to the praise houses. They could look forward to these occasional "Shouts" much as the young people of the white race look forward in most communities to their dances, but with this difference—the singing and the steps had a religious significance. Their churches still frown on dances, but the "Shouts" were born and live in the praise houses.

There should not be too fast a change in this custom, inevitable as it is to change. The young people of this generation to whom the motion picture has come, the play parties, the entertainments in church and Community House do not crave the "Shouts" as in the old days. They are likely to pass out with the fast changing conditions on the islands. But we should remember that they have served a real purpose in the lives of a rural people.

V

The young candidates for admission to the church must "come through" the praise house. In our community the "Seeker" must "see visions and dream dreams" which are interpreted to him by a "Spiritual Father" or a "Spiritual Mother," who is chosen after having been seen in a dream.

A "Seeker" is often marked by a white string tied around his head to show to the world that he should not be disturbed. He must not play games nor sing, and in the old days many were not allowed to go to school during this experience for fear the distractions would interfere with their praying. Wrote Caesar to his teacher: "I am not in school today. I guess you might know the reason. I am trying to join the Church and I don't want to develop my brain to so much things at a time." This meant sometimes that a pupil would miss so much in school that he lost his place in his class. Together with the ministers we worked out a plan that the "Candidates" might come to school but if they desired it, they could always be excused to go home early and by themselves, and they would not be expected to take part in the games.

I have known young people to go into the woods and stay on their knees for hours; and in the night or before "dayclean," to steal out for conference with their Spiritual Mothers or Fathers who try to lead them on from step to step in this great experience. Sometimes it takes a long time to see all that is required before the candidate is examined by the praise house leaders. Sometimes a candidate gets discouraged and "turns back"—a serious thing in his career.

The final meeting with the church deacons before baptism and communion is a formal examination. Then, if all is satisfactory, the "candidates" are ready for the great Sunday, which means to them and to all the people a newness of life and new responsibilities. The outward sign is the complete outfit of new clothes, and not even graduation at school can reach the climax attained by these young or old seekers of religion.

Never shall I forget the early baptism I attended one

summer morning. There was a large class, between sixty and seventy, old and young, for hearts had been touched by a comet in the sky which brought more closely the tremendous power of the Almighty. To our people the church is indeed an "Ark of Safety" and that morning there was a great gathering.

I had been told to be ready at six o'clock but the minister's boy knocked loudly on our door at four. The "tide did not suit" for so late a beginning as had been planned. We went out into the starlight to find the candidates in position and ready to march down to the river.

All were dressed in white, and as they marched, they sang. From the little bridge where we stood, we could see a few belated travelers in their white robes hurrying across the marsh to join the procession. The stars shone on the little winding tide river, now reaching far across the marshes. The palmettoes and live oaks near by were not more silent watchers than the friends who had gathered to see the candidates go down into the water. Two deacons went ahead to test its depth, the minister followed, but not until he had read the Scripture, offered a prayer, and given a short talk on the meaning of baptism to the Baptists. Then, two by two, the candidates stepped forth, and each one was plunged below the surface. When he came out of the water, a friend or a relative met him. One who is approved by the church is chosen and this is an honor. A quilt or a coat was thrown about the head and shoulders and off they drove as quickly as the small island ponies could travel.

As we stood there on the bridge, the red glow of the sunrise made the scene one of peculiar glory. Sidney Lanier in his matchless poem gives the picture:

The tide's at full: the marsh with flooded streams
Glimmers, a limpid labyrinth of dreams.
Each winding creek in grave entrancement lies
A rhapsody of morning stars. The skies . . .
Shine scant with one forked galaxy, . . .
The marsh brags ten; looped on his breast they lie . . .
And lo, in the East! Will the East unveil?
The East is unveiled, the East hath confessed
A flush: 'tis dead; 'tis alive: 'tis dead, ere the West
Was aware of it: nay, 'tis abiding, 'tis withdrawn:
Have a care, sweet Heaven! 'Tis Dawn.

Finally all were baptized. The little ones had come first in the procession. Now it was broad daylight. The preacher again offered a prayer and gave the benediction and we walked home through the live oaks, the brilliant sunshine making shadow pictures on the road. The ebb tide left only a narrow bit of a river in the wide stretch of marsh grass. To my mind came those other lines of Lanier's:

Run home, little streams
With your lapfulls of stars and dreams.

The formal acceptance into the church is only a final ceremony that crowns all the days and nights of praying, prayer interpretations, and the great act of the baptism. It is not unlike the ceremony of churches on the mainland.

VI

Seven Negro churches serve our island—one, the Brick church, with its old slave gallery now turned to other uses, an inheritance from the white congregation of plantation days. The others are of wood, and represent much effort and sacrifice on the part of their builders. They are the oldest and strongest organizations among a people who have had little experience in business enterprise and have no part in the political life of the region. And, save for Penn School, and the little county schools, they have been throughout the decades of freedom the institutions which have quickened the cultural life of the people as well as shepherded their ways. All of these churches are Baptist, with one exception—a little congregation that was planted here when some of the followers of Sherman's army, from an upcountry region where Methodism flourished, were settled on the island in war time. There is another exception, the overgrown crumbling walls of a Chapel of Ease, which in the pre-war days was tributary to the old vine-clad Episcopal church in Beaufort.

The churches must depend upon the people, and no one in our island church is too young to help in its support. The taking of the collection is indeed a feature in the service that means much to all who take part. Deacons take their place by the table. The preacher lines off the hymn, the singing begins, the congregation begins to move. All go forward to the table where change can be quickly made, if necessary. The congregation moves quietly—down one aisle and up the other is the rule when the crowd is large. People can see each other and can be seen. Sometimes a leader rises in his seat and leads a spiritual. Then the money comes faster as a rule. The rhythm helps those who were holding back. "Now will the Choir come down," calls out the minister, and that group so important to the church joins the procession, and are the last to put their gifts on the table. The amount is counted by the deacons in charge and is announced to the people.

There is great pride in the churches, and they are kept in good order. There has always been the closest coöperation between them and Penn School. Education and religion go together on St. Helena. As a going principle of our community work no new plan or policy is adopted before it has been aired in the churches. And together we have been working at breaking down many of the old superstitions. For superstition is of course the crudest expression of the religious feeling in all races. I have spoken of the "basket-names" given the children. When I asked a mother the reason for this she said, "So the evil one can't know the real name." Most of the mothers of today would not even know the foundation for the custom. And so we find Precious, Treasure, Stormy, Better Days, Golden Days, Worky, Husky, Handsome, Fortune, and other jolly good descriptive names, Nob, Morsel, and Nice, and the twins, Peas and Beans! When I found that one door of an island home was kept open even in cold weather and asked the reason, the answer was given that the good spirit might want to enter and should find the open door. When I asked why both doors were shut at night, the answer was that the old hag might come and draw out the first person to open the door. One of the older people told me of seeing spiders taken from his arm and leg by the conjure doctor and feeling much better after it! And occasionally we find a sick person who believes that his malady has been "laid on" him by an enemy.

These are remnants of things which must hark back to Africa and the East. But as the new leadership comes on, the old superstitions are passing. When we launched our health campaign against typhoid fever through the praise houses and the churches, we found much of the old fatalistic tendency: "If de Lord will you hab tarrify fever, you goin' to hab de tarrify fever. If he will you goin' to die—you a-goin' to die." But we found the churches fairly and squarely on the side of the sanitary measures being waged by the doctor and the school.

My belief is that religion is the gift of the Negro to our American life. There is its strong dramatic expression found in the praise houses on the plantations. It wells up through the songs of the race. The spirituals are their one articulate contribution, echoing the history of a people who have come through the valley of the shadow. In their prayers no less than their music do we find poetic imagery and spiritual values. I shall give Aunt Jane's prayer in full for it illustrates all I have been trying to say of the religion of these people. It was written down by Ellen Murray, one of the Founders of Penn School. She heard Aunt Jane give it in one of the island churches; and as it had said so much to her, she wanted to preserve it for others:

AUNT JANE'S PRAYER

Dear Maussuh Jesus, we all uns beg Ooner [you] come make us a call dis yere day. We is nuttin' but poor Etiopian women and people ain't t'ink much 'bout we. We ain't trust ask any of dem great high people for come to we church, but do' you is de one great Maussuh, great too much dan Maussuh Linkum, you ain't shame to care for we African people.

Come to we, dear Maussah Jesus. De sun, he hot too much, de road am dat long and boggy [sandy] and we ain't got no buggy, for send and fetch Ooner. But Maussuh, yo' 'member how yo' walked dat hard walk up Calvary and ain't weary but t'ink about we all dat way. We know you ain't weary for to come to we. We pick out de torns, de prickles, de brier, de backslidin' and de quarrel and de sin out of yo' path so dey shan't hurt Ooner pierce feet no mo'.

Come to we, dear Maussuh Jesus. We all uns ain't got no

good cool water for give yo' when yo' t'irsty. You know, Maussuh, de drought so long, and de well so low, ain't nuttin' but mud to drink. But we gwine to take de 'munion cup and fill it wid de tear ob repentence and love clean out ob we heart. Dat all we hab to gib yo', good Maussuh.

An' Maussuh Jesus, you say you gwine stand to de door and knock. But you ain't gwine stand at we door, Maussuh, and knock. We set de door plum open for yo' and watch up de road for see yo'.

Sisters [turning to the other women in the church], what for you-all ain't open de door so Maussuh know He welcome?

One woman rose quietly from her knees and set the church door wide.

Come Maussuh Jesus, come! We know you is near, we heart is all just tremble, tremble, we so glad for hab yo' here. And Maussuh, we church ain't good 'nuff for yo' to sit down in, but stop by de door jes' one minute, dear Maussuh Jesus, and whisper one word to we heart—one good word—we du listen —Maussuh.

And so on our "School Acres" mingle the old and the new. Education is a civilizing process and, in spite of the speed that has gripped this century, civilization is the slowest thing in the world. Here among our island folk life holds close to all that is best in the past, close to the rivers and to the soil, and to the sky; but it reaches out also to the practical things of a new age. In the old island phrase which hailed the dawn; we turn our faces toward "dayclean."

APPENDIX

I. SUMMARY OF INDUSTRIAL AND VOCA-TIONAL WORK AT PENN SCHOOL

The practical work for the girls is divided under six headings:

I. Housekeeping
   House cleaning
   Cooking
   Laundering
   Canning and preserving

II. Home Management
   Care and use of rooms
   House furnishings
   House decorations
   Planning meals
   Cooking meals
   Household accounts
   Labor-saving devices
   Taking monthly inventories
   Inspection and supervision of work of Groups I and II

III. Gardening
   Flowers, vegetables, fruit and nut trees
   The girls are divided into three clubs, working under different conditions:
      The Thrifty Workers
      The Thrifty Home Makers
      The Faithful Garden Workers

IV. Sewing
   Plain sewing
   Dressmaking
   Millinery

V. Library
   General care of the school library which serves the community and the school

VI. Practice Teaching
   Normal students, Grade XII

The practical work for the boys is divided under eleven headings:

    I. Farm fields and orchard
    II. Forestry and wood supply
    III. Dairy
    IV. Live stock
    V. Garden
    VI. Roads and grounds
    VII. Native island basketry
    VIII. Blacksmithing and wheelwrighting
    IX. Carpentry
    X. Cobbling, harness making, and upholstery
    XI. Machine repairs

II

The school year is divided into four terms, each about ten weeks in length. These terms follow the seasons, autumn, winter, spring, and summer. Work assignments are made for all high school girls and boys at the assignment meetings held on the Thursday preceding the beginning of the new term. The assignments are read in Chapel on the Friday before the new term.

III

The pupils are classified in three groups as follows:
Group I. Beginners, coming to the department for the first time and those failing to pass to Group II.
Group II. Dependables, who have shown ability to perform independently work assignments in the department.
Group III. Leaders, who can take responsibility in the department and supervise other pupils while working themselves.
    Each pupil before graduation is expected to attain

Group III in at least two departments and to have attained Group II in all departments to which he or she has been assigned for two terms.

IV

Records of the practical work are kept in a small looseleaf book, which is the property of the pupil. One sheet shows the divisions of work, the number of weeks spent in each division, the group made in each, the average grade, and on the back of that sheet the remarks made by the instructor, on the ability, initiative, neatness, trustworthiness, and leadership shown. Another sheet shows a summary for each department filled out at the end of each term. One sheet shows the departments with the date of starting the work and the date of ending given so a glance shows just how much time that pupil has spent in each, and this picture is of great value in showing work covered.

The pupils take their books when they leave school, but their records are also copied into a School Record Book.

V

Assignments are made according to the need and the qualifications of each pupil. It is an elastic system designed to meet the needs of the individual.

VI

The high school pupils are divided into two sections, alternating classroom studies and practical work in the morning and afternoon sessions.

VII

The industrial work for the elementary school begins with Grade V. Their work assignments are for the school year in two departments. One day a week is given to practical work.

VIII

Work at home is visited and "counted." The pupils are enrolled in clubs with their own officers, and a Junior Farmers' Fair in the autumn term serves to dramatize their work.

Note. Our appreciation for help in developing this plan is given to the American Farm School in Salonica, Greece, founded by Dr. and Mrs. John Henry House. We have adopted their general plan, adapting it to our island conditions.

INDEX